Catholicism Explained: A Clear G
for New Believers

Ariella Dawn

Introduction: Embracing the Faith

Understanding Catholicism: A Journey of Faith
Catholicism is not just a religion but a lifelong journey of discovery, transformation, and deepening relationship with God. For new believers, the process of embracing the Catholic faith can feel both exhilarating and overwhelming. This introduction serves as your first step into a rich tradition that spans over two thousand years, with a profound connection to the life and teachings of Jesus Christ. Catholicism is a faith of both personal and communal dimensions; it is about entering into an intimate relationship with God and living that out in the context of the Church and the world.

In this guide, we will walk you through the essentials of the Catholic faith, providing clarity on what it means to be a Catholic, what the Church teaches, and how these teachings apply to your everyday life. For some, Catholicism may be a familiar religion, but for others, it might feel entirely new. No matter where you are on your journey, the Church invites you to come and see, to learn, and to grow in the love of God.

Catholicism is rooted in the belief that God has revealed Himself to humanity through the person of Jesus Christ. Jesus' life, death, and resurrection are not just events of the past; they are ongoing realities that continue to shape and transform the lives of believers. The faith is not merely intellectual assent but a way of life, a relationship with God that shapes how we view the world, interact with others, and find meaning in our everyday lives.

The Purpose of This Guide
This guide is meant to be a clear and concise introduction to the Catholic faith, designed for those who are beginning their journey or seeking to deepen their understanding. It will answer the most common questions new believers may have, such as:

- What is the Church, and why is it important?

- What do Catholics believe about God, Jesus, and the Holy Spirit?
- How do the sacraments work, and why are they vital to Catholic life?
- What does it mean to live as a Catholic in the modern world?

By embracing the faith, you are not only joining a religious institution but entering a living, breathing community of believers who share the same faith, hope, and love in Christ. The Catholic Church is a universal family that transcends cultural, racial, and national boundaries. It is a diverse and vibrant community, with over 1.3 billion members around the world, united in the belief that Jesus Christ is Lord and that His Gospel is the truth for all people.

This guide will also introduce you to the historical and theological roots of Catholicism. From the earliest Christian communities that followed Christ's teachings, to the development of Church doctrine, the establishment of the sacraments, and the missionary efforts that spread the faith across the world, Catholicism has always been about one thing: following Christ. The goal is to equip you with the knowledge and understanding needed to not only embrace Catholicism but to live it with conviction and joy.

A Life of Faith, Hope, and Love

At its core, Catholicism is a call to live a life of faith, hope, and love. Faith in the belief that God is real, that He loves us, and that He revealed Himself to us through Jesus Christ. Hope in the promise of eternal life, that our present struggles are temporary and that God's kingdom is real and eternal. And love—love for God, for neighbor, and for all of creation.

In the coming chapters, we will explore the rich teachings and practices that shape a Catholic's spiritual life. But the foundation is always personal: a relationship with God that begins with a simple yet profound "yes." This "yes" is your act of faith, your willingness to respond to God's invitation to be in relationship with Him and with His Church.

Through the sacraments, prayers, and the guidance of the Church, this relationship will grow deeper. You will be nurtured spiritually, morally, and intellectually, called to participate in a faith that demands both personal commitment and active service to others. You will be called to live a life that reflects Christ's love and to carry that love into the world.

Why Catholicism?

In a world filled with choices and spiritual paths, why Catholicism? Why not one of the many other religions or philosophies? Catholicism offers a deep, rich, and life-giving relationship with God that is grounded in the historical reality of Christ's life and the teachings of the Apostles. The Catholic Church is a living continuation of the work Christ began, and it offers not just a set of beliefs, but a way of life that includes prayer, worship, sacraments, and a commitment to justice and peace.

Catholicism provides the fullness of the Christian faith, offering a robust theology that is both intellectual and experiential, sacramental and communal. It challenges its members to think critically, to serve others selflessly, and to strive for holiness in every aspect of life.

The beauty of Catholicism is that it invites everyone—no matter their background, education, or life experiences—into a deeper relationship with God. It doesn't just ask for intellectual agreement; it asks for transformation. It challenges us to live as disciples, to not only follow Christ in word but in deed, and to make His love visible to the world.

What's Next?

As you embark on your journey into the Catholic faith, this guide will give you the tools you need to explore and grow in your understanding of God's love. Each chapter will unpack important aspects of Catholic life, from the Church's beliefs to the sacramental life and moral teachings. You will discover not only what the Church teaches but why these teachings matter to you personally.

Whether you are coming from a background of faith or just starting to seek, the Catholic Church welcomes you. The faith is alive, and it is waiting for you to embrace it fully, with an open heart and mind. The journey may not always be easy, but it will be rewarding, leading you to a deeper understanding of God's love and the joy that comes with living out His commandments.

Chapter 1: The Foundations of Catholicism

Introduction to Catholicism

Catholicism, the largest Christian denomination in the world, is deeply rooted in the life, teachings, and mission of Jesus Christ. At its core, Catholicism is a faith centered on the belief that God has revealed Himself to humanity through Jesus Christ and that this revelation is preserved and transmitted through the Catholic Church. The foundations of Catholicism are built upon two key elements: **Sacred Scripture** (the Bible) and **Sacred Tradition** (the teachings and practices handed down through the Church), which are guided by the **Magisterium** (the teaching authority of the Church). Understanding these foundational aspects is crucial for anyone beginning their journey in the Catholic faith.

The Apostolic Origins of the Church

Catholicism traces its origins directly back to the Apostles, the twelve men chosen by Jesus to be His closest followers. After Christ's death and resurrection, these Apostles became the first leaders of the Christian community. The Catholic Church believes that Jesus established the Church on the foundation of these Apostles, and it continues to be guided by their teachings today.

The most pivotal moment in this apostolic foundation occurred when Jesus appointed Peter, one of the twelve, as the leader of the Church. In the Gospel of Matthew (16:18), Jesus says to Peter, "You are Peter, and on this rock I will build my church." This moment is understood by Catholics as the institution of the papacy, which is the office of the Pope, the spiritual leader of the global Church. The papacy, alongside the bishops and priests, forms the governing body of the Church, which carries the mission Christ entrusted to His Apostles: to preach the Gospel, baptize believers, and make disciples of all nations.

The Role of Sacred Scripture and Sacred Tradition

Catholicism is deeply anchored in both **Sacred Scripture** and **Sacred Tradition**, two pillars of the faith.

1. **Sacred Scripture** refers to the Bible, the inspired Word of God. Catholics believe that the Old and New Testaments, in their entirety, are divinely inspired and contain all that is necessary for salvation. However, the Catholic understanding of Scripture differs from that of many Protestant denominations. Catholics accept 73 books in the Bible, including the deuterocanonical books (or "Apocrypha"), which are not part of the Protestant canon. These books, such as Tobit, Judith, Wisdom, and 1 and 2 Maccabees, are included because the Catholic Church recognizes them as part of the true, inspired Word of God.

2. **Sacred Tradition** refers to the teachings, practices, and interpretations of Scripture that have been passed down from the Apostles through the centuries. Catholics believe that, alongside the Bible, Sacred Tradition is a living and essential source of divine revelation. Sacred Tradition includes the liturgy, Church doctrines, and the writings of the early Church Fathers—those men who were closest to the Apostles and who played a key role in interpreting and explaining the faith.

For Catholics, Sacred Scripture and Sacred Tradition are not two competing sources of revelation, but complementary. The Church teaches that the Bible cannot be fully understood apart from the context provided by Tradition, which helps to safeguard and interpret the Word of God. In this sense, the Catholic Church does not hold to "sola scriptura" (the belief that Scripture alone is authoritative), but rather holds that the Church, guided by the Holy Spirit, is entrusted with the responsibility to teach, preserve, and interpret both Scripture and Tradition.

The Role of the Magisterium

The **Magisterium** is the teaching authority of the Catholic Church, entrusted with the responsibility of interpreting both Sacred Scripture and Sacred Tradition. It is exercised by the Pope, as the successor of Saint Peter, and by the bishops in communion with him. The Magisterium ensures that the teachings of the Church remain faithful to the apostolic tradition and that they are applied to the lives of contemporary believers.

The Magisterium is not a source of revelation in itself, but rather serves as a guide to preserve and communicate the faith. The Pope, as the bishop of Rome, has a unique role as the leader of the Magisterium. He holds a special authority over the Church, ensuring that doctrine is taught faithfully and that the Church remains united in its beliefs. This authority is exercised in communion with the bishops, who, as successors of the Apostles, are the primary teachers of the faith in local communities. Together, the Pope and the bishops form the Magisterium.

Through the Magisterium, the Church can address contemporary issues and clarify the teachings of Christ in light of new challenges. For instance, in matters of moral theology, social issues, and doctrinal clarification, the Magisterium provides the definitive interpretation of Scripture and Tradition. Catholics believe that the Holy Spirit guides the Magisterium, ensuring that it remains faithful to Christ's teachings.

The Apostles' Creed and the Nicene Creed: Summary of Beliefs
The foundations of Catholicism are expressed succinctly in two important creeds: the **Apostles' Creed** and the **Nicene Creed**. These creeds are declarations of faith that summarize the core beliefs of Catholicism.

1. **The Apostles' Creed** is the oldest and most widely used Christian creed, attributed to the Apostles. It is a brief summary of the essential elements of Christian belief, including belief in God the Father, Jesus Christ the Son, and the Holy Spirit. The Creed is used in the Church's daily prayers, including during the recitation of the Rosary.

2. **The Nicene Creed** was formulated in 325 AD at the First Council of Nicaea to address various theological controversies of the time. It is a more detailed affirmation of the faith, particularly regarding the nature of Jesus Christ and the Holy Trinity. The Nicene Creed remains the standard profession of faith in Catholic Mass and is recited by Catholics worldwide during Sunday liturgies.

Both creeds encapsulate the core doctrines of Catholicism, including the belief in the Holy Trinity, the divinity and humanity of Jesus Christ, His death and resurrection, and the role of the Church in God's plan of salvation.

The Catholic Church: The Body of Christ

Catholics believe that the Church is not merely a human institution, but the **Body of Christ** on earth. This metaphor, found in St. Paul's letters, emphasizes that the Church is united in Christ and is called to continue His mission. The Church is both a **visible** institution and a **spiritual** reality, with Christ as its head and its members as the various parts of His Body. The Church exists to teach the Gospel, administer the sacraments, and serve the world through acts of charity and justice.

The Church's authority is not derived from human power but is rooted in the will of Christ, who established the Church to carry on His work. The Church is called to be a light to the nations, proclaiming the Good News of salvation and offering a path to holiness for all people. Catholics believe that, through the sacraments, the Church is the primary means by which individuals encounter Christ, particularly through the Eucharist, which Catholics believe to be the true Body and Blood of Christ.

The Foundation for a Life of Faith

In this chapter, we have explored the fundamental foundations of Catholicism: the apostolic origins of the Church, the role of Sacred Scripture and Sacred Tradition, the teaching authority of the Magisterium, and the creedal summaries of the Catholic faith. These foundations are essential for understanding Catholicism and living as a Catholic.

As a new believer, embracing these core elements is essential to growing in your faith. The Catholic Church invites you to be part of this rich, two-thousand-year-old tradition, which continues to be rooted in the person of Jesus Christ. Through the Church, you are invited to encounter Christ in a personal way, to be transformed by His grace, and to share His love with the world.

Chapter 3: The Sacraments: Channels of Grace

Introduction to the Seven Sacraments

The **Seven Sacraments** are one of the most significant elements of Catholicism, deeply embedded in the life of the Church and essential to the spiritual journey of every Catholic. These sacred rites are seen as powerful encounters with God's grace, through which believers are initiated into the life of the Church, strengthened in their faith, and helped to grow in holiness. The Sacraments are both signs and means of God's presence and action in the world. They are not merely symbolic rituals; they are believed to be effective channels of God's grace, transforming the lives of those who participate in them with faith.

The Seven Sacraments are categorized into three groups based on their purpose and the stage of Christian life they represent:

1. **Sacraments of Initiation**
2. **Sacraments of Healing**
3. **Sacraments of Service of Communion**

Each of the Seven Sacraments is a visible and tangible way for Catholics to experience God's love and mercy. The Catechism of the Catholic Church describes the Sacraments as the "ordinary means" by which God's grace is communicated to humanity. Through the Sacraments, Catholics believe they encounter Jesus Christ directly and are incorporated more fully into His Body, the Church. Let's take a closer look at the Seven Sacraments, which serve as the building blocks of a Catholic's spiritual life.

---

1. Baptism: The Gateway to the Christian Life

Baptism is the first and foundational Sacrament of initiation. It is through Baptism that a person is officially welcomed into the Church and begins their new life in Christ. Catholics believe that through Baptism, original sin is washed away, and the person is reborn as a child of God. Baptism also marks the beginning of a lifelong journey of faith.

Baptism is usually performed in infancy but can also be administered to adults who are converting to Catholicism. The Rite of Baptism involves the pouring of water over the head of the person (or full immersion, depending on the tradition), accompanied by the words, “I baptize you in the name of the Father, and of the Son, and of the Holy Spirit.”

The grace conferred in Baptism is a spiritual rebirth that initiates the individual into the communal life of the Church. It is a Sacrament that speaks to the promise of salvation and the call to a life of holiness, preparing the believer to receive the other Sacraments.

---

2. Eucharist: The Real Presence of Christ

The **Eucharist** is the central and most important Sacrament in Catholic life. Often referred to as the "source and summit" of the Christian faith, the Eucharist is celebrated at every Mass. Through the Eucharist, Catholics believe they are receiving the actual Body and Blood of Jesus Christ under the appearances of bread and wine.

Catholics believe that during the celebration of the Mass, the bread and wine are **transubstantiated**—that is, their substance changes into the Body and Blood of Christ, even though their outward appearances remain the same. This is known as the doctrine of the **Real Presence**. By receiving the Eucharist, Catholics believe they are participating in the Last Supper of Jesus with His disciples, and they are drawn into a deeper communion with Christ and one another.

The Eucharist nourishes the soul, strengthens the believer in their Christian walk, and grants grace that deepens the relationship between the believer and God. It is also a Sacrament of thanksgiving, for it allows the faithful to give thanks to God for the gift of salvation won through the life, death, and resurrection of Jesus.

---

3. Confirmation: The Strengthening of the Holy Spirit

Confirmation is the second Sacrament of Initiation, following Baptism. It is a Sacrament in which the baptized person receives the **Holy Spirit** in a deeper way, empowering them to live out their Christian faith boldly and witness to Christ in the world.

During Confirmation, the bishop (or priest, in certain circumstances) anoints the person with **holy chrism** (a mixture of oil and balsam) and says, "Be sealed with the gift of the Holy Spirit." This anointing marks the individual with the Holy Spirit's presence, a sign of strength, courage, and sanctification. Confirmation also deepens the grace received at Baptism, strengthening the person to be an active and mature member of the Church.

It is a Sacrament that helps the believer grow in their relationship with the Holy Spirit, enabling them to bear witness to Christ and live their faith more fully in their everyday lives. In many dioceses, Confirmation is traditionally administered to adolescents, but adults who are baptized and wish to become full members of the Church also receive this Sacrament.

---

4. Penance (Reconciliation): Healing and Forgiveness

Penance, also called **Reconciliation** or **Confession**, is the Sacrament of healing where Catholics confess their sins to a priest and receive absolution, restoring them to a state of grace. This Sacrament is rooted in the belief that sin damages one's relationship with God and the Church. Through the Sacrament of Penance, Catholics experience God's mercy, receive forgiveness for their sins, and are reconciled with the Church community.

The process of confession involves the penitent (the person confessing) admitting their sins to the priest, who acts in the person of Christ and offers forgiveness. The priest will often give a penance, a prayer or action that the person must perform to help repair the damage caused by their sin. Through this Sacrament, Catholics are reminded of God's infinite mercy and the importance of humility, repentance, and reconciliation with others.

---

5. Anointing of the Sick: Comfort and Healing

The **Anointing of the Sick** is a Sacrament of healing, administered to those who are seriously ill, elderly, or near death. It offers spiritual and physical healing through the laying on of hands and anointing with holy oil. This Sacrament is intended to provide comfort, strength, and peace, especially during times of suffering or at the approach of death.

The Anointing of the Sick is not limited to the final moments of life but is available to anyone facing serious health challenges. It is a way for the individual to experience God's healing presence and to be strengthened in the face of illness. Catholics believe that through this Sacrament, the sick person can be spiritually healed, and, in some cases, physical healing may also occur as part of God's divine will.

---

6. Matrimony: The Vocation of Love

Matrimony, or **Marriage**, is a Sacrament that unites a man and woman in a lifelong, loving, and faithful bond. Catholic teaching holds that marriage is a vocation—a calling from God—and that the couple, through the Sacrament, becomes a living sign of Christ's love for the Church.

In the wedding ceremony, the couple exchanges vows before a priest or deacon, who represents the Church, and makes a promise to love and serve each other as Christ loves His Church. Matrimony is a Sacrament that signifies the unity and sacrificial love of Christ for His people, as well as the partnership that exists between a husband and wife. It is also ordered toward procreation, as the couple is called to bring new life into the world, nurturing and raising children in the faith.

---

7. Holy Orders: The Priesthood of Christ

Holy Orders is the Sacrament through which men are ordained as deacons, priests, or bishops, to serve the Church and its members. Through Holy Orders, a man receives the grace and authority to perform certain sacraments (such as the Eucharist, Penance, and Anointing of the Sick) and to lead the Christian community in faith.

The Sacrament of Holy Orders continues the apostolic mission of Jesus, who called twelve men to be His closest companions and entrusted them with the mission of preaching the Gospel and administering the sacraments. Catholic teaching holds that the ordained clergy are acting in the person of Christ, and through them, the Church is able to carry on its sacred mission.

The Seven Sacraments are the lifeblood of Catholic spiritual practice. Through these Sacraments, Catholics experience God's grace in real and tangible ways. They form the foundation of the Church's teaching and are essential to the believer's spiritual journey, helping them grow in holiness, deepen their relationship with God, and serve others in the world. Each of the Sacraments plays a specific and necessary role in the life of the faithful, guiding them from the beginning of their Christian life to the end. Together, the Sacraments are the means by which Catholics come to understand and live out the love, mercy, and salvation offered by God through Jesus Christ.

Baptism: The Gateway to the Christian Life

Baptism is the first and foundational Sacrament of the Christian life. It marks the beginning of the journey of faith, welcoming individuals into the Catholic Church and initiating them into the divine life of God. Baptism is the gateway through which a person is spiritually reborn, cleansed from original sin, and incorporated into the Body of Christ. For Catholics, Baptism is not just a rite of passage but a profound spiritual transformation, through which one enters into a personal relationship with God and the community of the Church.

The Significance of Baptism

Baptism holds a central place in Catholic theology and practice, because it is the key to salvation. In the Gospel of John (3:5), Jesus tells Nicodemus, "Very truly I tell you, no one can enter the kingdom of God unless they are born of water and the Spirit." This phrase emphasizes the necessity of Baptism for entry into the kingdom of God and eternal life.

Baptism is also the Sacrament that removes original sin, the state of separation from God inherited from Adam and Eve. Catholic teaching holds that every human being is born with original sin, and through Baptism, this sin is washed away, enabling the person to be reconciled with God and to begin a new life of grace. It is through this purification that an individual becomes a member of the Church, the family of God, and is given the opportunity to grow in holiness.

In addition to cleansing from sin, Baptism signifies a deeper reality of being **reborn** into the life of Christ. As St. Paul writes in Romans 6:4, "We were therefore buried with him through baptism into death in order that, just as Christ was raised from the dead through the glory of the Father, we too may live a new life." Through Baptism, Catholics believe that they participate in the death and resurrection of Jesus, spiritually dying to their former selves and rising to a new life in Him.

The Rite of Baptism

The Rite of Baptism is a visible, symbolic act that represents the spiritual reality occurring. It generally consists of the following elements:

1. **Water** – The most important symbol of Baptism is the water used in the rite. Water represents purification, renewal, and rebirth. It symbolizes the washing away of sin and the new life that is conferred by God's grace. Water is poured over the head of the person being baptized, or in some traditions, the person is fully immersed in the water, symbolizing the death of the old self and the rising to a new life in Christ.

2. **The Trinitarian Formula** – The Catholic Church teaches that Baptism must be performed using the Trinitarian formula: "I baptize you in the name of the Father, and of the Son, and of the Holy Spirit." This is an essential part of the rite because it affirms the central doctrine of the Holy Trinity, which is foundational to Catholic theology. Through this formula, the baptized person is initiated into the life of the Triune God—Father, Son, and Holy Spirit.

3. **The Sign of the Cross** – The priest or deacon traces the sign of the cross on the forehead of the person being baptized, signifying the person's identity with Christ and marking them as a member of His Body, the Church.

4. **Anointing with Chrism** – After Baptism, the newly baptized person is anointed with **chrism** (a holy oil), which signifies the gift of the Holy Spirit. Chrism is a symbol of being set apart for God's service, and it strengthens the person to live as a member of Christ's Body, the Church.

5. **White Garment** – The newly baptized person is often given a white garment, symbolizing the purity of the new life they have received in Christ. This garment is a visible sign of their spiritual transformation and the grace they have received.

6. **Candle** – A lit candle is given to the newly baptized, representing the light of Christ. This is a reminder that the person, now a

member of the Church, is called to live in the light of Christ and to be a witness to His Gospel in the world.

Baptism of Infants and Adults

In the Catholic Church, Baptism is administered both to **infants** and to **adults**, depending on the circumstances and the faith background of the individual.

1. **Infant Baptism** – Catholicism has a long tradition of baptizing infants, and the Church believes that this practice is deeply rooted in Scripture and tradition. Infants, even though they are not capable of personal sin, are baptized to cleanse them from original sin and to initiate them into the Church. The parents and godparents make the promises on behalf of the child, committing to raise the child in the Catholic faith. This is why godparents play a significant role in the sacrament—they are called to assist the parents in fostering the child's spiritual growth.

2. **Adult Baptism** – For adults who are converting to Catholicism, Baptism is an integral part of the Rite of Christian Initiation of Adults (RCIA). In this process, adults are prepared to receive Baptism, along with the other Sacraments of Initiation—Confirmation and Eucharist—during the Easter Vigil. Adult Baptism involves a period of catechesis (instruction) in the faith, culminating in the reception of the Sacrament, which is usually accompanied by a public profession of faith.

Baptism and the Church Community

Baptism is not just an individual act—it is a communal event that integrates the baptized person into the family of the Church. The Church is not just a collection of individual believers; it is a living, breathing community, the Body of Christ. Through Baptism, the baptized person becomes a member of this community, sharing in the same mission and responsibilities.

Catholic teaching stresses that Baptism is the foundation of a life of faith, and it commits the believer to a life of worship, service, and holiness. As members of the Church, the baptized are called to participate in the Eucharist, engage in prayer, serve others, and follow Christ's commandments. Baptism also calls the faithful to bear witness to their faith, helping to spread the Good News of Jesus Christ to the world.

Baptism and Salvation

Catholic doctrine teaches that Baptism is necessary for salvation. In the words of Jesus, "No one can enter the kingdom of God unless they are born of water and the Spirit" (John 3:5). While the Catholic Church recognizes the possibility of salvation for those who have not been baptized, it teaches that Baptism is the normative way by which God offers His grace and salvation to the world. This belief is rooted in the words of Christ and the early Church's practices.

For Catholics, Baptism is not merely an optional or symbolic act—it is a necessary and powerful Sacrament through which God's saving grace is conferred. It is the beginning of a new life in Christ, marked by grace, holiness, and a mission to live out the teachings of Jesus in the world.

Baptism is the gateway to the Christian life, the first step in the journey of faith. Through this Sacrament, the baptized person is cleansed from sin, reborn into a new life in Christ, and initiated into the Church community. Baptism marks the beginning of a lifelong journey of conversion, grace, and holiness. It is the foundation for all the other Sacraments and the source of a believer's relationship with God. For both infants and adults, Baptism is a sign of God's great love and an invitation to live a life dedicated to Him. It is the moment when a person becomes a child of God and a member of His Church, ready to grow in faith, receive God's grace, and share His love with the world.

Eucharist: The Real Presence of Christ

The **Eucharist**, also known as the **Holy Communion**, is the central act of worship in Catholicism and is considered the "source and summit" of the Christian life. It is the Sacrament that draws Catholics into intimate communion with Jesus Christ Himself, nourishing them spiritually and strengthening their faith. Through the Eucharist, Catholics believe they receive the **real presence** of Jesus Christ—Body, Blood, Soul, and Divinity—under the appearances of bread and wine. This profound mystery, celebrated at every Mass, represents the heart of Catholic spirituality, bringing the believer into direct contact with Christ's saving grace.

The Eucharist is not merely a symbol; Catholics believe in the doctrine of **transubstantiation**, which holds that during the celebration of the Mass, the bread and wine truly become the Body and Blood of Christ, while retaining the appearance of bread and wine. This belief emphasizes the **real presence** of Christ in the Eucharist and its central role in the life of every Catholic.

The Institution of the Eucharist

The origins of the Eucharist are found in the **Last Supper**, the final meal Jesus shared with His disciples before His Passion. During this meal, which took place on the night before His crucifixion, Jesus instituted the Eucharist. In the Gospels of Matthew, Mark, and Luke, we read that Jesus took bread and wine, blessed them, and said, "This is my body... this is my blood... do this in memory of me" (Luke 22:19-20, Matthew 26:26-28, Mark 14:22-24). Through these words, Jesus transformed the bread and wine into His own Body and Blood, commanding His disciples to continue this act in His memory.

Catholics believe that through these words, Jesus instituted the Eucharist as a perpetual Sacrament for the Church. This action was not merely a symbolic gesture, but a profound mystery in which Jesus gave Himself completely to His followers. The Eucharist is both a **memorial** (a living remembrance of Jesus' death and resurrection) and a **sacrifice** (the actual presentation of Christ’s Body and Blood for the salvation of the world). Through the Eucharist, the Church participates in the eternal sacrifice of Jesus on the cross, making present the reality of His passion, death, and resurrection in the here and now.

The Real Presence of Christ

The doctrine of the **Real Presence** is the foundation of the Catholic understanding of the Eucharist. Catholics believe that during the celebration of the Mass, the bread and wine are **transubstantiated**, meaning that their substance is completely changed into the Body and Blood of Christ, while their appearance remains unchanged. The Catholic Church teaches that Christ is truly present—Body, Blood, Soul, and Divinity—in the Eucharist.

This is not a symbolic presence or a mere representation, but a true, substantial presence of Christ. The Church teaches that the Eucharist is the same Body and Blood that was given up for the salvation of humanity on the cross. Therefore, every time the Eucharist is celebrated, it is not a reenactment or remembrance of Christ's sacrifice, but the **actual** sacrifice of Christ being made present to us.

The presence of Christ in the Eucharist is both mysterious and profound. While the bread and wine retain the physical appearance of bread and wine, they are no longer merely ordinary substances; they have been transformed into the very Body and Blood of Jesus. As Jesus Himself said in John 6:56, "Whoever eats my flesh and drinks my blood remains in me, and I in them." This powerful statement emphasizes the intimate communion that occurs between the believer and Christ through the reception of the Eucharist.

The Role of the Priest and the Mass

The Eucharist is celebrated within the context of the **Mass**, the central act of Catholic worship. The priest, acting in the person of Christ (in persona Christi), consecrates the bread and wine, calling down the Holy Spirit to transform them into the Body and Blood of Christ. This is done through the **Words of Consecration**, which echo the words of Jesus at the Last Supper: "This is my body... This is my blood..." (Matthew 26:26-28).

The priest's role is crucial because, as the ordained minister of the Church, he serves as the instrument through which Christ acts in the celebration of the Eucharist. The priest does not change the bread and wine by his own power but is the vessel through which Christ's power works. This sacramental act is also a communal one, as the faithful, gathered together as the Body of Christ, share in this sacred meal, receiving Christ's Body and Blood, and offering themselves in return.

In the Mass, the faithful participate in the **Liturgy of the Word** (where the Scriptures are proclaimed) and the **Liturgy of the Eucharist** (where the bread and wine are consecrated and distributed). The Mass is a thanksgiving offering, a **sacrifice of praise**, in which the Church offers Christ to the Father, just as He offered Himself for us on the cross. The Eucharist is a means of worship and communion, a sacred bond between God and His people.

The Benefits of Receiving the Eucharist

The Eucharist is a source of grace and spiritual nourishment for the Catholic believer. By partaking of the Eucharist, Catholics believe they are drawn into a deeper union with Christ and the Church. The Catechism of the Catholic Church teaches that the Eucharist strengthens the believer to live a life of holiness, fortifies them against sin, and helps them to grow in love for God and neighbor.

1. **Union with Christ** – Through the Eucharist, Catholics are intimately united with Christ. The Eucharist is a foretaste of the heavenly banquet, where believers will be fully united with God for all eternity. By consuming Christ's Body and Blood, the faithful are spiritually nourished and united with the life of God.

2. **Spiritual Nourishment** – Just as food nourishes the body, the Eucharist nourishes the soul. Catholics believe that the Eucharist provides the spiritual strength necessary to face the challenges of daily life and to remain faithful to God's commandments. It is a source of grace that empowers the believer to live according to Christ's teachings.

3. **Forgiveness of Sin** – The Eucharist also serves as a means of **spiritual healing**. While the Sacrament of Penance is specifically

for the forgiveness of mortal sins, the Eucharist forgives **venial sins** (lesser sins) and strengthens the soul against temptation. Regular reception of the Eucharist is seen as a way to remain in a state of grace, continually growing in holiness.

4. **Strength for Christian Life** – Through the Eucharist, Catholics are strengthened to live out their vocation as disciples of Christ. The Eucharist enables believers to become more like Christ in their words, actions, and attitudes, giving them the grace to live selflessly and to serve others, especially in times of suffering and hardship.

The Eucharist and the Church

The Eucharist is not only an individual sacrament but a **communal** one. When Catholics gather to celebrate the Eucharist, they do so as the Body of Christ. The Mass is an expression of the unity of the Church, as all the members of the Church, from the clergy to the laity, participate in the same sacred act. In receiving the Eucharist, believers are drawn into deeper communion with one another, strengthening the bonds of the Church.

The Eucharist also forms the foundation for the Catholic Church's mission in the world. The Eucharist is a pledge of future glory, a sign of the unity that Christians are called to embody, and a source of strength for carrying out Christ's work of evangelization and service to the world. By receiving the Eucharist, Catholics are sent out to be Christ's hands and feet, serving others and sharing the Good News of salvation.

The Eucharist is the heart of Catholic worship, offering believers the opportunity to encounter Christ in a profound and transformative way. Through the Eucharist, Catholics experience the **real presence** of Christ, participate in His sacrifice, and receive the spiritual nourishment necessary for the Christian journey. It is not just a ritual; it is the **Source and Summit** of the Christian life, the very life of Christ made available to all who believe. The Eucharist is both a gift and a mystery, calling all who partake to grow in union with Christ and with one another, living out the love that Christ has shown to the world.

Confirmation, Penance, and Anointing of the Sick

While **Baptism** and the **Eucharist** are the foundational Sacraments of Christian initiation, **Confirmation**, **Penance**, and the **Anointing of the Sick** are equally vital in the life of a Catholic. Each of these Sacraments deepens the believer's relationship with God, fortifies them spiritually, and equips them for their mission in the world. These Sacraments serve to **strengthen** (Confirmation), **heal** (Penance), and **comfort** (Anointing of the Sick) believers as they navigate the challenges of the Christian journey.

---

1. Confirmation: The Strengthening of the Holy Spirit

Understanding Confirmation

Confirmation is the second Sacrament of initiation, following Baptism, and it is the Sacrament in which a person receives a deeper outpouring of the Holy Spirit. While Baptism cleanses a person from original sin and makes them a member of the Church, Confirmation strengthens them to live out their faith in the world. Confirmation is sometimes referred to as the "Sacrament of maturity" because it empowers the individual to take on a more active role in the Church and in their personal relationship with God.

The Rite of Confirmation

During the celebration of Confirmation, the bishop (or priest, in some cases) anoints the forehead of the confirmand (the person being confirmed) with chrism (a consecrated oil) and says, "Be sealed with the Gift of the Holy Spirit." The laying on of hands and the anointing signify the reception of the Holy Spirit, who strengthens the individual to be a witness to Christ.

The effects of Confirmation are profound and lasting. The confirmed person receives the fullness of the Holy Spirit, who empowers them to live out the Christian vocation with courage and conviction. The Seven

Gifts of the Holy Spirit—wisdom, understanding, counsel, fortitude, knowledge, piety, and fear of the Lord—are especially important and serve to guide the individual in their spiritual growth. Confirmation also deepens the relationship with God, enabling the believer to bear fruit in their personal and communal life.

---

2. Penance (Reconciliation): Healing and Forgiveness

Understanding Penance

The Sacrament of Penance (also known as Reconciliation or Confession) is the Sacrament of healing. It is through Penance that Catholics seek forgiveness for their sins and are reconciled with God and the Church. Sin, both mortal and venial, disrupts a person's relationship with God and the Church, and through this Sacrament, the individual experiences God's mercy and is restored to grace.

The Need for Reconciliation

Catholic teaching emphasizes that while Baptism removes original sin, Christians still struggle with sin throughout their lives. This struggle can be particularly damaging in the case of mortal sin, which separates the person from God. However, **venial sins**, while not destructive to the soul's state of grace, still weaken the relationship with God and hinder spiritual growth. Regular participation in the Sacrament of Penance offers the faithful an opportunity for reconciliation with God and the Church, cleansing the soul, and empowering the individual to continue their journey of faith.

The Rite of Penance

The process of receiving Penance typically involves the following steps:

1. **Examination of Conscience** – The penitent reflects on their sins and prepares themselves to confess them.

2. **Confession** – The penitent confesses their sins to a priest, who acts in the person of Christ (in persona Christi).

3. **Penance** – The priest assigns a penance, which may consist of prayers, acts of charity, or some other task designed to help the penitent atone for their sins.

4. **Absolution** – The priest then absolves the penitent of their sins by saying the words of absolution: "I absolve you from your sins in the name of the Father, and of the Son, and of the Holy Spirit."

Through this Sacrament, Catholics are reminded of God's infinite mercy and the need for constant repentance and renewal. The Sacrament of Penance also strengthens the believer against future temptation and empowers them to live in a way that reflects Christ's love and holiness.

The Grace of Penance

The grace conferred by the Sacrament of Penance brings healing and restoration. It forgives mortal and venial sins, strengthens the individual's will to avoid sin, and promotes the sanctification of the soul. It also reconciles the penitent to the Church, as sin disrupts the communion between the individual and the Church community. Penance restores that communion, ensuring that the person is fully reintegrated into the Body of Christ.

---

3. Anointing of the Sick: Comfort and Healing

Understanding Anointing of the Sick

The Anointing of the Sick is the Sacrament that offers comfort, healing, and strength to those who are suffering from illness, injury, or the frailty of old age. It is a Sacrament of healing, but not necessarily of physical healing. Catholics believe that, through this Sacrament, God provides spiritual healing, peace, and the grace needed to endure suffering. It is often received by those preparing for surgery, experiencing serious illness, or nearing death.

The Rite of Anointing of the Sick

The Anointing of the Sick involves the anointing of the forehead and hands of the sick person with holy oil (chrism or the oil of the sick) by a priest, while praying for the person's healing, both physically and spiritually. The priest prays that the person may be healed in body, soul, and spirit, and that they may be given the strength to face their illness or suffering with peace and courage.

The grace conferred through this Sacrament is not only intended for physical healing but also for the healing of the soul. It provides spiritual strength and peace, comforting the person in the face of fear and anxiety, particularly at the end of life. For those who are seriously ill, Anointing of the Sick also provides a spiritual preparation for death, helping the individual to surrender themselves peacefully to God's will.

When Should the Anointing of the Sick Be Received?

The Anointing of the Sick is not only for those near death. It can be received by anyone who is seriously ill, facing surgery, or experiencing a long-term or chronic illness. It is important to note that this Sacrament can be received multiple times, particularly if the person's condition worsens or if they experience a relapse in their health.

For those nearing death, the Anointing of the Sick is a powerful act of God's presence, offering peace, comfort, and preparation for the final journey. It is often accompanied by the **Viaticum** (the Eucharist for the dying), which is the "food for the journey" as the person prepares to pass into eternal life.

The Grace of Anointing of the Sick

The grace conferred by the Anointing of the Sick is multifaceted:

1. **Healing and Comfort** – The Sacrament offers physical and spiritual healing. While physical healing is not guaranteed, the anointing strengthens the soul and provides peace, which helps individuals endure their suffering and find courage in their trials.

2. **Union with Christ's Suffering** – The suffering experienced in illness or old age can be united with Christ's own suffering on the cross, thus giving meaning to the individual's suffering and allowing them to participate in the redemptive work of Christ.

3. **Preparation for Death** – For those at the end of life, the Anointing of the Sick prepares them for the transition from this life to the next, offering the peace that comes from knowing God's loving presence in the midst of life's final moments.

Together, the Sacraments of **Confirmation**, **Penance**, and the **Anointing of the Sick** play crucial roles in a Catholic's spiritual life. **Confirmation** strengthens the believer to live as a witness to Christ and to carry the mission of the Church into the world. **Penance** provides healing and forgiveness, restoring the individual to God's grace and enabling them to live a more faithful life. **The Anointing of the Sick**, with its healing, comfort, and preparation for death, ensures that believers are never alone in their suffering and that God's presence remains with them, especially in their weakest moments.

Matrimony: The Vocation of Love

Matrimony, also known as **Marriage**, is one of the Seven Sacraments of the Catholic Church and is considered a sacred covenant between a man and a woman. It is a vocation—meaning it is a divine calling—not just a social contract or a legal arrangement. The Catholic Church teaches that marriage is a **reflection of Christ's love for the Church**, marked by mutual self-giving, faithfulness, and love. Through the Sacrament of Matrimony, a man and woman are united in a lifelong partnership, not only for their own mutual benefit but also for the good of society and the Church.

In Matrimony, two individuals freely choose to commit their lives to one another, fostering a relationship based on love, respect, and the desire to help each other grow in holiness. Catholic teaching emphasizes that the marriage relationship is meant to be a **sign of God's love**—a love that is **total, faithful, fruitful**, and **self-giving**. Matrimony is both a **personal covenant** between the couple and a **sacramental sign** that reveals God's loving presence in the world.

Theological Foundations of Matrimony

The Divine Origin of Marriage

Marriage has its origins in the very creation of humanity. In the **Book of Genesis**, God declares, "It is not good for the man to be alone. I will make a helper suitable for him" (Genesis 2:18). From the beginning, God intended human beings to live in communion with one another, and marriage is the institution through which this communion is most fully expressed. The Catholic Church teaches that marriage was established by God not only for companionship but also for the procreation and education of children, as well as the mutual sanctification of the spouses.

In the New Testament, Jesus Himself affirms the sanctity of marriage. In the Gospel of Matthew, Jesus says, "What God has joined together, let no one separate" (Matthew 19:6). By this, Christ elevates marriage to a

Sacrament, giving it a sacred and indissoluble nature. The Church teaches that **marriage is a sacrament** because Christ Himself instituted it and graces the union with His presence, sanctifying the couple and their relationship.

The Sacrament of Matrimony: A Sacred Covenant

The Vocation of Love

Marriage in the Catholic Church is viewed as a **vocation of love**, where the spouses are called to love each other as Christ loves the Church. The **vocation of love** is more than just an emotional or romantic feeling; it is a total, lifelong commitment to the other person, characterized by sacrificial love, faithfulness, and the desire for the good of the other. This love mirrors Christ's love for His Church, which is unconditional and selfless.

In his letter to the Ephesians, St. Paul writes: "Husbands, love your wives, just as Christ loved the Church and gave Himself up for her" (Ephesians 5:25). This call for husbands to love their wives as Christ loved the Church is a profound challenge, one that requires men and women in marriage to embrace sacrifice, service, and mutual respect. The love between a married couple is not just for their own benefit but also for the witness it gives to the world about God's love.

A Permanent and Indissoluble Bond

Matrimony, as a Sacrament, creates an **indissoluble bond** between the husband and wife. This means that the couple is not simply in a temporary relationship but is united permanently. Jesus taught that marriage is a lifelong commitment, and the Church teaches that the bond created by Matrimony is unbreakable by human authority. The Sacrament of Matrimony gives the couple the grace to live out their vows and to persevere through the challenges of life together.

The **indissolubility** of marriage is one of the key aspects of Catholic teaching, meaning that, except in cases of a **valid annulment** (a declaration by the Church that the marriage was not valid from the start), no civil or ecclesiastical authority can dissolve a marriage. This teaches the dignity and permanence of the marital relationship and the importance of fidelity in marriage.

The Twofold Purpose of Matrimony

The Catholic Church teaches that there are two essential purposes of marriage:

1. **The Unitive Purpose** – Marriage is designed to unite the couple in a deep, loving, and intimate bond. The unitive purpose emphasizes the personal relationship between husband and wife, highlighting love, mutual support, companionship, and the sharing of life. The couple is called to help each other grow in holiness, support one another's dreams and ambitions, and build a life together based on mutual respect and love.

2. **The Procreative Purpose** – Marriage is also oriented toward **procreation**, or the having and raising of children. The Church teaches that children are a gift from God and that marriage provides the proper context for their upbringing. A married couple is entrusted with the responsibility to nurture, educate, and form their children in the faith. Catholic teaching emphasizes that the **openness to life** is essential in marriage, meaning that spouses are called to welcome children as gifts and to cooperate with God's plan for human life. This aspect of marriage stresses the family as the domestic Church, where parents are the first teachers of the faith.

These two purposes—**unity** and **procreation**—are complementary. While the love between spouses is central, the Church also stresses the importance of marriage as the natural and proper context for raising children in a stable, loving environment.

The Rite of Matrimony

The Celebration of the Wedding

The Sacrament of Matrimony is celebrated through the **wedding ceremony**, which is often a joyful and public event. During the ceremony, the couple exchanges vows in the presence of the priest (or deacon), who acts as the Church's official witness. The exchange of vows is the moment when the couple freely and intentionally commits to each other for life, saying words such as, "I take you to be my wife/husband, to have and to hold, from this day forward, for better, for worse, for richer, for poorer, in sickness and in health, to love and to cherish, until death do us part."

The couple's consent, freely given, is the key element in the validity of the marriage. This consent is what makes the marriage a sacrament, and without it, the marriage cannot be recognized by the Church. The Church believes that this exchange of vows, made before God and the community, is an act of faith and trust, which forms the foundation for the couple's new life together.

The Blessing of the Rings

The wedding rings are often blessed during the ceremony, symbolizing the couple's commitment and fidelity to one another. The rings are exchanged as a visible sign of the covenant they are making, reminding them of their permanent bond. The **ring**, being a circle with no end, symbolizes the eternal nature of the love and commitment they share.

The Grace of Matrimony

The Spiritual Strength of Marriage

Matrimony is not just a natural institution but also a Sacrament that bestows special grace upon the couple. This grace helps the couple live out their vocation, grow in holiness, and navigate the challenges and struggles of life. Through this grace, spouses are strengthened to fulfill their mutual responsibilities—love, support, and care for each other, as well as to raise children in the faith. The grace of Matrimony also helps spouses to persevere in love, especially during difficult times, and to remain faithful to their vows, even when tested by the trials of life.

The Church teaches that marriage is a path to holiness, and through the love shared between the couple, they both encounter Christ. The marriage relationship is an avenue for each spouse to grow in virtue and to love more selflessly, as Christ loved the Church.

Matrimony is one of the most profound and beautiful Sacraments in the Catholic Church. It is a **vocation of love**, in which the couple is called to imitate Christ's self-sacrificial love for His Church. Through the Sacrament of Matrimony, a man and a woman are united in a lifelong covenant that is both personal and sacred, with the call to be open to life and to raise children in the faith. Matrimony is not just a contract but a **sacramental sign** of God's eternal love, a love that is total, faithful, fruitful, and self-giving. It is a relationship that invites both spouses to grow in holiness, to serve one another, and to reflect the love of God to the world.

Holy Orders: The Priesthood of Christ

Holy Orders is the Sacrament through which the mission entrusted by Christ to His Apostles is continued in the Church. It is through this Sacrament that men are consecrated and set apart for a special role of service to the Church and the people of God. The priesthood, the most commonly known form of Holy Orders, is the way in which Christ Himself remains present in the world, administering His grace to the faithful through the Sacraments, preaching, and pastoral care. In Catholic theology, Holy Orders encompasses three levels: **deacon**, **priest**, and **bishop**, each with its own unique role in the life of the Church.

Holy Orders is not merely an honor or a position of power; it is a calling to serve as a **mediator** between God and humanity. The priesthood, in particular, is seen as the **priesthood of Christ**, in which ordained ministers act in persona Christi (in the person of Christ) to offer worship, dispense grace, and lead others into deeper communion with God.

The Priesthood of Christ

The Eternal Priesthood of Christ

The priesthood established by Christ is eternal and unchanging. Jesus, as both God and man, is the **eternal High Priest** who offers Himself as the perfect sacrifice for the forgiveness of sins. In the letter to the Hebrews, it is written, “For we do not have a high priest who is unable to sympathize with our weaknesses, but we have one who has been tempted in every way, just as we are—yet he did not sin. Let us then approach God’s throne of grace with confidence” (Hebrews 4:15-16). Christ’s priesthood is unique because He is both the Priest and the Sacrifice.

In His earthly ministry, Jesus ordained the Apostles to continue His work of preaching the Gospel and offering the Sacrament of the Eucharist, symbolizing His Body and Blood. By doing so, He established the foundation of the priesthood in the Church. He said to His Apostles, "Do this in remembrance of me" (Luke 22:19), commanding them to offer the Eucharist in His name and to continue the mission He began. Through the **Sacrament of Holy Orders**, this priesthood is passed on to the clergy, who act in the person of Christ, especially in the celebration of the Eucharist.

The Priest as Mediator
The priest is called to act as a mediator between God and humanity, just as Christ did. He offers prayers and sacrifices on behalf of the people, interceding for them before God. The priesthood is not about personal glory but about service—serving God and serving the people by bringing them into a closer relationship with Christ. This is most evident in the celebration of the **Eucharist**, where the priest consecrates the bread and wine into the Body and Blood of Christ, making present Christ's sacrifice on the cross.

The Three Degrees of Holy Orders

Holy Orders consists of three distinct levels: **deacon**, **priest**, and **bishop**. Each level is a step in the development of the priestly ministry and plays a vital role in the Church's mission.

1. The Diaconate (Deacon)

The **deacon** is the first level of Holy Orders. Deacons are ordained to serve the Church in various capacities, including assisting at Mass, preaching, administering certain Sacraments (such as Baptism and marriage), and performing works of charity. The deacon's role is one of service to the community, reflecting Christ's example of servant leadership.

Deacons do not have the power to consecrate the Eucharist or offer absolution in Confession, but they do assist in the liturgical and pastoral work of the Church. Their primary vocation is to serve the people of God, particularly the poor, the sick, and those in need. Deacons are called to imitate Christ's humility and self-sacrificial love through service, which is a hallmark of Christian leadership.

2. The Priesthood (Priest)

The **priest** is the second degree of Holy Orders. Priests are ordained to serve the Church in the role of the **Sacramental Minister**, celebrating the Eucharist, hearing Confessions, anointing the sick, and performing other Sacramental duties. Through the **Sacrament of Holy Orders**, priests receive the authority to offer the Eucharist and to preach the Word of God.

A priest acts **in persona Christi**, meaning he stands in the place of Christ in his priestly ministry. This is most evident in the celebration of the Eucharist, where the priest, speaking in the person of Christ, consecrates the bread and wine into His Body and Blood. By doing so, the priest continues Christ's work of salvation, making Christ present to the people through the Sacraments.

Priests are also called to shepherd their parish communities, offering pastoral care, counseling, and support to those in need. They guide their parishioners in their spiritual lives, helping them grow in faith and holiness. Priests are often called to lay down their lives for their flock, emulating the self-giving love of Christ.

3. The Episcopacy (Bishop)

The **bishop** is the highest degree of Holy Orders. Bishops are the successors of the Apostles and have the fullness of the Sacrament of Holy Orders. They are entrusted with the responsibility of overseeing the **entire Church**, particularly within a diocese. Bishops have the authority to ordain deacons, priests, and other bishops, ensuring the continuation of the priestly ministry. They are the primary teachers, governors, and sanctifiers in the Church.

A bishop's role is not only to serve the local community but to ensure the faithful transmission of the Church's teaching and the proper administration of the Sacraments. They act as shepherds, guiding their flock with wisdom, authority, and compassion. Bishops are also called to be the **witnesses** of unity in the Church, particularly in communion with the Pope, who is the Bishop of Rome and the leader of the universal Church.

The Rite of Holy Orders

The **Rite of Holy Orders** is a profound liturgical celebration that takes place during Mass. The Sacrament is administered through the laying on of hands, a gesture that signifies the conferral of the Holy Spirit's power and the grace necessary for the ordained person to carry out their ministry.

The Laying on of Hands
The **laying on of hands** is an essential part of the Rite of Holy Orders. It is through this gesture that the bishop imparts the gift of the Holy Spirit, which enables the candidate to act in the person of Christ. The laying on of hands is an ancient practice that symbolizes the transmission of authority and grace.

The Prayer of Consecration
During the ceremony, the bishop recites the **prayer of consecration**, asking God to bestow the gifts and graces necessary for the individual to fulfill their role. This prayer emphasizes that the ordained are receiving a mission from God to serve His people and to bring His grace to the world.

The Vesting
The newly ordained priest, deacon, or bishop is vested in sacred vestments, which symbolize their sacred role. The deacon receives a **stole** and **dalmatic**, the priest receives the **stole** and **chasuble**, and the bishop is vested with the **mitre** and **crozier**, signifying his role as a shepherd of the Church.

The Grace of Holy Orders

Holy Orders confers a special **sacramental grace** that empowers the ordained to fulfill their role in the Church. The grace of this Sacrament is not only a personal gift but also one that benefits the entire Church. Through this grace, the ordained are enabled to:

- **Preach the Word of God** with authority and truth.
- **Celebrate the Sacraments** faithfully and effectively, particularly the Eucharist, where they make Christ present to His people.
- **Offer spiritual guidance** and pastoral care, helping others grow in holiness and fulfill their own vocations.
- **Lead the people of God** in holiness, helping them grow in faith and overcome the challenges of life.

For priests and bishops, this grace helps them to live out their vocation of sacrificial service, to remain faithful to their vows of celibacy, and to be witnesses of Christ's love and mercy in the world.

Holy Orders is a sacred and transformative Sacrament that continues the work of Christ in the world. Through the **priesthood of Christ**, ordained ministers are set apart to serve the Church, administer the Sacraments, and lead others to deeper communion with God. In the **laying on of hands** and the prayer of consecration, the grace of the Holy Spirit is conferred, empowering the ordained to fulfill their mission as **mediators**, **teachers**, and **shepherds**. This Sacrament emphasizes the Church's belief that **service** in the name of Christ is at the heart of the Christian vocation, and those ordained are called to live out this mission with humility, faithfulness, and love.

Sacramentals and Devotional Practices

In addition to the Seven Sacraments, which are central to Catholic life, the Church also recognizes **sacramentals** and **devotional practices** as important means of growing in faith, deepening one's relationship with God, and living out the Christian vocation. Sacramentals are sacred signs and objects that the Church uses to encourage the faithful to be open to God's grace and to foster spiritual growth. They are distinct from the Sacraments but are connected to them because they help sanctify the believer and lead them to the ultimate goal of salvation.

Devotional practices, which are deeply embedded in the daily life of the Catholic Church, also serve as means for strengthening one's spirituality and devotion to God. These practices are not strictly necessary for salvation but are powerful ways to deepen faith and foster a strong relationship with God.

---

1. Sacramentals: Sacred Signs and Objects

What Are Sacramentals?
Sacramentals are **sacred signs** instituted by the Church to sanctify different circumstances in human life. They include a variety of objects, prayers, blessings, and actions that, while not conferring grace in the same way the Sacraments do, help individuals prepare to receive God's grace and offer daily opportunities for spiritual growth. Unlike the Seven Sacraments, which are instituted by Christ, sacramentals are instituted by the Church.

Sacramentals draw the faithful to God by making visible the invisible realities of divine life and salvation. They are signs of God's presence and can be used to bless both people and things, invoking divine protection, healing, or guidance.

Types of Sacramentals
Sacramentals take many forms. They include:

1. **Blessings** – Special prayers or rituals that consecrate or dedicate a person, place, or thing to God. For example, the blessing of homes, religious articles (like rosaries), or animals.

2. **Holy Water** – Water that has been blessed by a priest. It is often used to bless oneself or a space, serving as a reminder of baptism and a symbol of purification.

3. **Rosaries and Crucifixes** – Objects used in prayer and devotion. The rosary is especially used for the recitation of the **Hail Mary** prayers, meditating on the mysteries of Christ's life. Crucifixes serve as visual reminders of Christ's sacrifice and love.

4. **Medals and Statues** – Sacred objects that symbolize a person or event in the faith, such as medals of saints or statues of the Holy Family. These objects help believers focus on particular aspects of the faith, serving as visible reminders of the holy people and events they represent.

5. **Candles** – Often blessed and lit during prayer, candles are symbols of Christ as the **Light of the World**. They are frequently used during prayer, especially during Mass, Advent, or funerals.

6. **Sacred Oils** – Used in the administration of several Sacraments, sacred oils (like chrism) are also used in blessings and anointings.

The Power of Sacramentals

While sacramentals do not confer grace in the same way the Sacraments do, they are efficacious in that they dispose the believer to receive God's grace. Sacramentals have an important role in sanctifying everyday life. Through them, Catholics invoke God's blessing and seek to be filled with His presence in all areas of life. For example, using holy water to bless one's home is a reminder of God's protection and sanctity. The act of carrying or wearing a medal of a saint serves as both a physical and spiritual connection to that saint, and the act of lighting a candle during prayer can symbolize one's prayers rising to God.

It is important to remember that sacramentals do not work automatically; their power comes from God's grace and the faith of the person using them. They are not magic; rather, they are spiritual tools to help individuals open their hearts to God's presence.

---

2. Devotional Practices: Deepening Faith Through Daily Prayer

What Are Devotional Practices?

Devotional practices are prayers, actions, or rituals that help Catholics focus on particular aspects of their faith and grow closer to God. While not required by the Church in the same way that the Sacraments are, devotions help to nurture a personal relationship with God. These practices often involve a repeated commitment to prayer and reflection, enabling the believer to live out the Gospel in practical and profound ways.

Devotions can range from private personal prayer to communal acts of worship and devotion. Many devotions are **Marian** (related to the Virgin Mary), while others focus on saints, certain aspects of Christ's life, or specific events in the liturgical year.

Popular Catholic Devotions

1. **The Rosary**
   One of the most well-known devotional practices in the Catholic Church is the **Rosary**. The Rosary is a prayer of meditation, focusing on the life of Jesus Christ and His Mother, Mary. Through the recitation of the **Hail Mary** prayers, the faithful meditate on the **Mysteries of the Rosary**, which include the key events of Christ's birth, death, and resurrection. The Rosary is a powerful tool for reflecting on the core mysteries of salvation and invoking the intercession of Mary.

2. **Adoration of the Blessed Sacrament**
   Eucharistic Adoration is a devotional practice in which the Blessed Sacrament (the Eucharist) is displayed for worship

outside of Mass. Catholics spend time in quiet prayer before the Eucharist, adoring the Real Presence of Christ. This practice deepens one's connection to Christ, strengthening the soul and drawing the believer into closer communion with God.

3. **The Stations of the Cross**
   The **Stations of the Cross** is a devotional practice, particularly during Lent and Holy Week, in which Catholics reflect on the key moments of Christ's Passion. Traditionally, 14 stations are observed, representing significant events in Christ's journey to His crucifixion, from His condemnation to His burial. This practice helps Catholics to meditate on Christ's suffering and sacrifice, fostering greater empathy, gratitude, and devotion to Him.

4. **Novena Prayers**
   A **novena** is a form of prayer offered over a period of nine days, either for a particular intention or in devotion to a saint or event. Novenas are often prayed with a specific prayer or set of prayers, and Catholics may pray them in times of need or in preparation for a feast day. Common novenas include those to the Holy Spirit (Pentecost), the Sacred Heart of Jesus, and specific saints such as St. Therese of Lisieux.

5. **Litanies**
   A **liturgy of supplication**, or **litanies**, is a form of prayer involving a series of invocations and responses, often asking for the intercession of saints or invoking God's mercy and protection. The **Litany of the Saints**, which lists saints by name and asks for their intercession, is a popular example. Litanies can be used for personal prayer or during Mass and other liturgical services.

6. **First Fridays and First Saturdays**
   The practice of devotion on the **First Friday of each month** (honoring the Sacred Heart of Jesus) and the **First Saturday of each month** (honoring the Immaculate Heart of Mary) is a form of reparation and devotion that many Catholics observe. These devotions were promoted by private revelations to saints such as St. Margaret Mary Alacoque and Sister Lucia of Fatima. They

involve attending Mass, receiving Holy Communion, and praying certain prayers on these days.

---

3. The Role of Sacramentals and Devotions in Daily Life

Sacramentals and devotions serve as everyday tools for **spiritual growth**. They provide tangible ways to express faith, keep one's mind focused on God, and integrate faith into everyday life. They are a means by which Catholics can make their whole life a **sacrifice of praise** to God, constantly returning to Him through prayer, reflection, and reverence.

For example:

- **Sacramentals** such as holy water or medals may be used to bless and sanctify personal spaces and possessions, turning daily routines into moments of divine awareness.
- **Devotional practices**, such as reciting the Rosary, praying before a crucifix, or attending Eucharistic Adoration, help believers center their lives around God's love, fostering peace and focus.

In times of struggle, **devotions** and **sacramentals** provide a way to offer prayers for oneself, others, and the world. They are a powerful means of participating in the larger life of the Church and helping the faithful grow closer to Christ and His Mother.

Sacramentals and devotional practices are integral aspects of Catholic life. While the Seven Sacraments are the primary channels of grace, sacramentals and devotions provide vital support in the spiritual journey. They are tools of sanctification and growth, leading Catholics toward a deeper connection with God and a more profound understanding of His love. Whether through the use of holy water, the daily recitation of the

Rosary, or participation in Eucharistic Adoration, these practices encourage Catholics to live their faith actively and continuously, transforming the ordinary into the extraordinary through the grace of God.

Chapter 4: Prayer and Worship in Catholic Life

The Mass: The Heart of Catholic Worship

The **Mass** is the central act of worship in the Catholic Church, the pinnacle of the Christian life. It is a celebration of **God's love**, **Christ's sacrifice**, and the **community of believers** coming together to be nourished by the Word of God and the Eucharist. The Mass is not merely a ritual or a form of spiritual practice—it is the living **re-presentation of the sacrifice of Christ** on the Cross. In the Mass, Catholics participate in the **Paschal Mystery**—the life, death, and resurrection of Jesus—uniting their own lives with Christ's self-sacrifice, receiving His grace, and being strengthened to live their faith in the world.

The Mass is the source and summit of the Christian life, where the faithful gather to worship, to receive the body and blood of Christ in the Eucharist, and to offer their lives in union with His. It is at the Mass that Catholics fully encounter the presence of Christ in both the **Word** and the **Eucharist**, making it the heart of their faith and the center of their worship.

The Structure of the Mass

The Mass is divided into two main parts: the **Liturgy of the Word** and the **Liturgy of the Eucharist**. These two parts work together to facilitate a complete experience of worship, where Catholics listen to God's word, respond in prayer, and receive Christ's body and blood to nourish them for the week ahead.

1. The Liturgy of the Word

The first part of the Mass is dedicated to the **Liturgy of the Word**, where the faithful listen to the sacred Scriptures, reflect on them, and respond to God's message through prayers and hymns.

- **The Entrance Rite** – The Mass begins with the procession of the priest, deacon, and altar servers, accompanied by the opening hymn. This signifies the assembly coming together as the Body of Christ.

- **The Penitential Rite** – After the opening prayer, the priest invites the congregation to reflect on their sins and ask for God's forgiveness, saying, "Lord, have mercy." The congregation then prays the **Gloria** in praise of God's holiness and mercy.

- **The Readings from Scripture** – The Scriptures are proclaimed from the **Old Testament** (on Sundays and feast days), **the Psalms** (sung or recited), the **Epistles** (letters from the New Testament), and **the Gospel**. These readings provide nourishment for the soul, offering guidance, inspiration, and correction for the Christian life.

- **The Homily** – Following the readings, the priest or deacon delivers the **homily**, a reflection on the Scriptures, helping the faithful to apply the Word of God to their lives. The homily serves to deepen the understanding of the teachings of the Church and encourage the congregation in their journey of faith.

- **The Profession of Faith** – After the homily, the congregation recites the **Nicene Creed**, affirming their belief in the core doctrines of the Catholic faith. The Creed is a declaration of unity, expressing shared belief in the Father, Son, and Holy Spirit, as well as in the Church's teachings.

- **The Prayer of the Faithful** – The Mass concludes the Liturgy of the Word with the **Prayer of the Faithful** (or Universal Prayer), where the congregation prays for the Church, the world, the sick, the dead, and any specific intentions. This is a moment of intercession, where the Church expresses its care for all of God's creation.

2. The Liturgy of the Eucharist

The second part of the Mass is the **Liturgy of the Eucharist**, the central focus of Catholic worship. It is during this part of the Mass that Catholics experience the **real presence of Christ** in the **Eucharist**—the consecrated bread and wine which, through the words of the priest, become the **Body and Blood of Christ**. The Liturgy of the Eucharist involves several key rituals:

- **The Preparation of the Gifts** – In this portion, bread, wine, and water are brought to the altar, signifying the offering of the faithful's lives and their work in the world. The priest offers these gifts to God, asking for His blessing. The gifts of bread and wine represent the fruits of creation and human labor, which are offered back to God in thanksgiving.

- **The Eucharistic Prayer** – The Eucharistic Prayer is the most solemn part of the Mass. The priest prays in **thanksgiving** for God's works, remembering Christ's saving acts, particularly His **Passion**, **Death**, and **Resurrection**. This prayer culminates in the **Consecration**, where the priest says the words of Christ from the Last Supper: "This is my Body... This is my Blood..."

  Through these words, the bread and wine are transformed into the **Body and Blood of Christ**. This is known as the **doctrine of transubstantiation**, which teaches that, though the appearances of bread and wine remain, their substance has changed into Christ's true Body and Blood. This moment is the **culmination** of the Mass and the **greatest mystery** of the Christian faith—the **Real Presence** of Christ in the Eucharist.

- **The Lord's Prayer** – After the Eucharistic Prayer, the congregation recites the **Our Father**, which is a prayer taught by Christ Himself. This prayer calls for God's kingdom to come and for His will to be done on earth as it is in heaven.

- **The Sign of Peace** – The priest invites the faithful to offer each other a sign of peace, symbolizing the unity of the Body of Christ. This is a reminder that before receiving the Eucharist, we must be reconciled with one another, as well as with God.

- **The Lamb of God** – The congregation prays the **Lamb of God** (Agnus Dei), asking Christ to have mercy on them and grant them peace. This prayer recalls the sacrifice of Christ, the true Lamb of God who takes away the sins of the world.

- **The Reception of Communion** – The faithful approach the altar to receive the **Body and Blood of Christ** in the Eucharist. Communion is the spiritual high point of the Mass, where Catholics receive Christ Himself, uniting with Him in a profound and intimate way.

- **The Concluding Rite** – The Mass ends with a final prayer, a blessing, and a dismissal. The priest dismisses the congregation with the words, "Go in peace, glorifying the Lord by your life." This reminds the faithful that their worship does not end with the Mass but continues in the world, as they carry Christ's love and presence to others.

The Significance of the Mass

The Mass is **central to Catholic life** because it is the ultimate form of worship. It is a **sacrifice**, a **banquet**, and a **communal act of praise and thanksgiving**. Through the Mass, Catholics:

- **Offer the sacrifice of Christ** to the Father: The Mass re-presents the sacrifice of Jesus on the Cross in an unbloody manner, making it present again for us. The Mass is not a new sacrifice but the same one that Christ made for our salvation.

- **Receive the Eucharist**, which is the very **Body and Blood of Christ**: Catholics believe that through receiving the Eucharist, they are nourished spiritually, grow in unity with Christ, and are strengthened to live out their faith.

- **Participate in the Paschal Mystery**: The Mass is a way for Catholics to unite themselves with Christ's death and resurrection, joining their own struggles, sufferings, and joys with His.

The Mass is also an expression of **community**. It is where the Church gathers to **pray, to give thanks, and to be fed spiritually**, strengthening the Body of Christ. The Eucharist unites all Catholics—past, present, and future—into one community, transcending time and space.

The **Mass** is the heart of Catholic worship because it connects believers directly with the mystery of **Christ's life, death, and resurrection**. It is a Sacrifice, a meal, and a communal act that nourishes the faithful and unites them with Christ. Through the **Liturgy of the Word** and the **Liturgy of the Eucharist**, the faithful are fed both spiritually and physically, and are sent forth to live their faith in the world. The Mass is more than a ritual; it is the life of the Church, a continual renewal of the **Paschal Mystery**, and the source from which all other aspects of Catholic life flow.

Personal Prayer: Connecting with God

Personal prayer is the most intimate and personal way Catholics connect with God. While the Mass, liturgical prayers, and sacramental practices are essential to the communal life of the Church, personal prayer is the **individual's direct dialogue with God**. Through prayer, a believer cultivates a relationship with the Creator, expresses gratitude, seeks guidance, and opens their heart to God's love and will. Personal prayer is not only about **asking** God for things but also about **listening** to Him, offering praise, and developing a deeper relationship with the divine.

For Catholics, personal prayer is an essential practice for spiritual growth and holiness. It's the foundation for a deeper faith, providing the grace and strength to live out God's will in daily life. It can take many forms, from structured prayers such as the **Our Father** to spontaneous, heartfelt conversations with God. No matter the method, the goal is always to draw closer to God, listen to His voice, and become more like Christ in love, service, and holiness.

The Importance of Personal Prayer

Building a Relationship with God
Prayer is fundamentally about relationship. Just as humans build relationships through communication, we connect with God through prayer. Personal prayer is an invitation to **spend time with God**—whether in silence, conversation, or meditation—allowing Him to speak to our hearts and guide our lives. It is in prayer that we open ourselves to God's presence, allowing Him to shape our thoughts, desires, and actions according to His will.

Jesus Himself modeled a life of prayer. Throughout the Gospels, we see Jesus frequently retreating to quiet places to pray to His Father. Whether in the wilderness, in the garden of Gethsemane, or on the mountaintop, Christ made prayer a priority. He spent time in personal prayer not only to seek God's guidance but to deepen His relationship with His Father. As His followers, Catholics are called to imitate this example and make personal prayer an essential part of their lives.

Spiritual Nourishment and Strength
Personal prayer is a source of spiritual **nourishment**. It is a way to recharge the soul, just as eating nourishes the body. In prayer, Catholics can receive the strength they need to face the challenges of daily life, find peace in the midst of turmoil, and experience God's healing touch. Prayer is a means of **resting in God's presence** and drawing from His grace.

Catholics are encouraged to pray when they are anxious, sad, joyful, or grateful. The Bible teaches that God is near to those who call upon Him, and that He hears the cries of His people (Psalm 34:18). Personal prayer provides a safe space to express **emotions, fears, desires, and gratitude** to God, knowing that He listens attentively and lovingly to every prayer.

Forms of Personal Prayer

There are many ways to pray personally, depending on individual preferences, circumstances, and needs. These forms of prayer can be formal or informal, structured or spontaneous. Here are some common types of personal prayer:

1. Vocal Prayer

Vocal prayer involves speaking words to God. It can be **formal**, like the **Our Father** or **Hail Mary**, or **spontaneous**, coming from the heart in the moment. Vocal prayer is often accompanied by physical gestures, such as kneeling or raising hands, to signify reverence and humility. The beauty of vocal prayer is that it can be prayed out loud, in your mind, or in silence, depending on the situation.

Examples of vocal prayer include:

- **The Lord's Prayer** (Our Father): A prayer taught by Jesus, expressing praise to God and requesting His guidance, mercy, and provision.
- **Hail Mary**: A prayer of devotion to the Blessed Virgin Mary, seeking her intercession.
- **Spontaneous Prayers**: Prayers spoken from the heart, such as asking God for strength in difficult times, offering thanks, or seeking guidance.

2. Meditative Prayer

Meditative prayer is a form of personal prayer where a person reflects on the **Word of God**, a particular mystery of faith, or an aspect of life in the presence of God. In this form of prayer, the mind and heart are actively engaged in trying to understand God's Word more deeply. It's an invitation to contemplate God's action in the world and in one's life.

Catholics often meditate on **Scripture** or **the Mysteries of the Rosary**, thinking about the significance of each event in Christ's life and how it applies to their own journey of faith. Meditation allows one to enter into the mind of Christ and discern His will more clearly.

Examples include:

- **Lectio Divina** (Divine Reading): A prayerful, meditative reading of Scripture where the believer reads, reflects, responds, and rests in God's Word.
- **The Rosary**: Meditating on the life of Christ through the events of the Rosary, contemplating the deep spiritual significance of His birth, death, and resurrection.

3. Contemplative Prayer

Contemplative prayer is the most silent and receptive form of prayer. In contemplation, a person simply rests in the **presence of God**, without words or thoughts, allowing God to fill their hearts with peace and love. This form of prayer emphasizes **listening** rather than speaking. It's an open and trusting encounter with God, a time to experience His closeness and His love.

Contemplation is the highest form of prayer, where the soul is still and fully receptive to God. It is often described as a form of **union with God**, a moment of deep peace where the person simply rests in His love.

Contemplative prayer can be difficult at first, as it requires training the mind to be still and attentive to God's presence. However, over time, it becomes a source of profound spiritual renewal and transformation.

4. Prayer of the Heart

The **prayer of the heart** is a personal and simple prayer form where the individual repeats a short, heartfelt prayer, such as **"Jesus, I trust in You"** or **"Lord, have mercy"**, over and over again. This type of prayer helps to keep the focus on God throughout the day and can be done in any setting, whether at home, in work, or on the go.

The **Jesus Prayer** (repeating "Lord Jesus Christ, Son of God, have mercy on me, a sinner") is a well-known prayer of the heart used in the Eastern Christian tradition. It's a simple, repetitive prayer that helps to center the soul on God and can be especially useful in times of distraction or stress.

The Role of Silence in Personal Prayer

Silence is a key element in personal prayer, particularly in **meditative** and **contemplative** prayer. In our fast-paced world, filled with noise and distractions, silence allows us to tune out external disturbances and focus entirely on God. Silence is the space where God's presence can be deeply felt. It is in the quiet moments of prayer that the heart becomes more receptive to God's voice.

In the Bible, we often see God speaking in **whispers** or stillness—whether through **Elijah** in the cave (1 Kings 19:12) or Jesus withdrawing to pray in solitude. Silence in prayer is not just the absence of sound, but an opening of the soul to hear God's gentle voice.

Why Personal Prayer Matters

Personal prayer is an essential part of the Catholic spiritual life because it provides a space for believers to grow in intimacy with God. Prayer is not just about **asking for things** but about **listening**, **adoring**, and **seeking** God's will. In personal prayer:

- We **open our hearts to God** and build a relationship with Him.
- We **reflect on God's Word**, allowing it to shape our thoughts and actions.
- We **seek God's guidance** in our decisions and seek His grace for the challenges of life.
- We **find peace** and comfort in His presence, especially in times of difficulty or sorrow.

Personal prayer allows the individual to enter into a **personal encounter with God**, which is the foundation for a deeper life of faith. Just as two friends deepen their relationship by spending time together, so too, a Christian's relationship with God deepens through personal prayer.

Personal prayer is the foundation of the Christian life, offering Catholics the opportunity to **connect with God** on a deeply personal level. Whether through vocal prayer, meditation, contemplation, or silent listening, personal prayer is the means by which individuals come into God's presence, seek His guidance, and offer their lives back to Him. In prayer, Catholics open their hearts to receive grace, find peace, and grow in holiness. Personal prayer is a continuous journey of **communion** with God, where believers are drawn into a deeper, more intimate relationship with the Creator, being transformed by His love and grace.

The Role of the Rosary and Other Devotions

Catholic devotions, such as the **Rosary**, play an essential role in the spiritual life of the Church. While the **Sacraments** are the primary channels of grace, devotions provide additional ways for Catholics to deepen their relationship with God and grow in holiness. These practices, particularly the Rosary, have been an integral part of Catholic life for centuries, drawing believers closer to the mysteries of Christ's life, death, and resurrection. Through these devotions, Catholics not only honor God and the saints but also seek spiritual strength, intercession, and a deeper understanding of their faith.

The Rosary, in particular, is a powerful prayer that invites the faithful to meditate on the central events of salvation history while reciting prayers such as the **Hail Mary** and **Our Father**. But the Rosary is just one example of a rich tradition of devotions that can lead believers to greater intimacy with God, assist in their spiritual battles, and help them live out their faith in daily life.

---

1. The Rosary: A Meditation on the Life of Christ

The Importance of the Rosary

The **Rosary** is one of the most popular and powerful devotions in Catholicism. This simple yet profound prayer is often described as a "compendium" of the Gospel, offering a way for Catholics to reflect on the most significant events in the life of Jesus Christ and His Mother, Mary. The Rosary consists of the recitation of prayers, mainly the **Hail Mary**, the **Our Father**, and the **Glory Be**, as well as the meditation on the **Mysteries of the Rosary**, which include the Joyful, Sorrowful, Glorious, and Luminous Mysteries.

The Rosary helps the believer to enter into a deeper contemplation of the mysteries of Christ's life, bringing them into a personal relationship with Jesus through the intercession of Mary. By meditating on these mysteries, Catholics grow in their understanding of the redemptive work of Christ and the love of His Mother, who is the ultimate model of faith and obedience.

The Mysteries of the Rosary

The **Mysteries of the Rosary** are the focal points of meditation while praying the Rosary. These mysteries are moments in the life of Christ and Mary that Catholics reflect upon to deepen their faith and grow closer to God. Each set of Mysteries invites the faithful to ponder specific events that reveal God's saving love for humanity.

- **Joyful Mysteries** (Focus: The birth and early life of Christ)
    1. The Annunciation
    2. The Visitation
    3. The Nativity
    4. The Presentation of Jesus in the Temple
    5. The Finding of Jesus in the Temple
- **Sorrowful Mysteries** (Focus: The Passion of Christ)
    1. The Agony in the Garden
    2. The Scourging at the Pillar
    3. The Crowning with Thorns
    4. The Carrying of the Cross
    5. The Crucifixion and Death of Jesus
- **Glorious Mysteries** (Focus: The Resurrection and glory of Christ)

1. The Resurrection
2. The Ascension
3. The Descent of the Holy Spirit
4. The Assumption of Mary
5. The Coronation of Mary as Queen of Heaven

- **Luminous Mysteries** (Focus: The public ministry of Christ)

    1. The Baptism of Jesus
    2. The Wedding at Cana
    3. The Proclamation of the Kingdom of God
    4. The Transfiguration
    5. The Institution of the Eucharist

By meditating on these mysteries, the Rosary helps to keep Christ at the center of daily life. The repetition of prayers provides a rhythm that facilitates focus, allowing the mind and heart to enter into the mystery being contemplated. This method of prayer aids the faithful in becoming more aware of God's actions in the world and in their own lives.

The Power of the Rosary

The Rosary has been described as a spiritual weapon because of its power to combat sin, strengthen the soul, and foster holiness. Catholics believe that Mary, as the **Mother of God**, intercedes on behalf of the faithful, and that praying the Rosary invites her help in our spiritual journey. In times of difficulty, the Rosary is a powerful prayer for comfort, healing, and strength.

Through the Rosary, Catholics not only seek spiritual growth and inner peace but also honor the life of Mary. She is seen as the perfect model of faith, trust, and obedience to God. The Rosary allows Catholics to connect with Mary in a personal and intimate way, asking for her prayers and intercession to guide them closer to Christ.

---

2. Other Catholic Devotions: Deepening the Faith

While the Rosary is perhaps the most well-known devotion, there are many other **devotional practices** in the Catholic tradition that assist in the faithful's spiritual journey. Each of these practices offers a unique way to connect with God, honor the saints, and strengthen one's relationship with the divine. Here are some of the most cherished devotions in Catholicism:

Devotion to the Sacred Heart of Jesus

The **Sacred Heart** of Jesus devotion emphasizes the love and mercy of Christ. It centers on the heart of Jesus as a symbol of His burning love for humanity. Catholics who practice this devotion often engage in the **First Friday devotions**, which involve attending Mass and receiving Holy Communion on the first Friday of each month, as well as praying specific prayers to the Sacred Heart.

The devotion reminds Catholics of Christ's infinite love and mercy, urging them to respond with their own acts of love and compassion. The Sacred Heart of Jesus is often depicted in art as a heart surrounded by thorns, pierced with a spear, and radiating light—symbolizing the deep suffering Christ endured for the sake of humanity.

Devotion to the Immaculate Heart of Mary

The **Immaculate Heart of Mary** represents Mary's pure love and total devotion to God. This devotion is closely related to the Sacred Heart of Jesus, as both devotions emphasize love, mercy, and obedience to God. Catholics who practice this devotion often pray the **First Saturday devotions**, attending Mass, receiving Communion, and offering prayers to Mary on the first Saturday of each month in reparation for sins.

The Immaculate Heart is depicted as a heart surrounded by roses, signifying purity and grace. Devotees are encouraged to model their own hearts after Mary's—the heart of a mother, obedient to God's will, full of love for all of humanity.

The Stations of the Cross

The **Stations of the Cross** is a devotional practice that invites the faithful to walk with Christ through His Passion, from His condemnation to His burial. This devotion is particularly popular during **Lent** and **Holy Week**, as Catholics reflect on Christ's suffering and sacrifice. The devotion consists of 14 "stations," or stops, each representing a moment in the Passion of Christ, such as His being condemned to death, His carrying of the cross, and His crucifixion.

Praying the Stations of the Cross encourages Catholics to meditate on Christ's immense love for humanity and the suffering He endured for salvation. It is a powerful means of growing in gratitude for the gift of redemption and becoming more deeply united with Christ.

Devotion to the Eucharist

Eucharistic devotion involves deep reverence and adoration for the **Body and Blood of Christ** present in the **Eucharist**. This devotion is often expressed through **Eucharistic Adoration**, where Catholics spend time in front of the Blessed Sacrament, praying and reflecting on Christ's real presence. Eucharistic Adoration is a powerful way to deepen one's relationship with Christ, recognize His presence in daily life, and grow in love and reverence for the Eucharist.

Catholics also observe **Corpus Christi**, a feast day dedicated to the Body of Christ, to publicly honor and give thanks for the gift of the Eucharist.

---

3. The Role of Devotions in Daily Life

Catholic devotions serve as practical means of cultivating a **deeper spiritual life**. They help keep God at the center of daily life, encouraging the faithful to take time out of their busy routines to pray, reflect, and worship. Whether through the Rosary, Eucharistic Adoration, or devotions to the Sacred Heart, devotions provide an opportunity for personal sanctification, spiritual growth, and deeper intimacy with God.

These practices also foster a **community spirit**. Many devotions are prayed collectively in parishes, where Catholics gather to meditate, pray, and offer their intentions for the Church and the world. Devotions strengthen the bond of fellowship among believers, who join together in common prayer and worship.

The **Rosary** and other Catholic devotions are rich spiritual practices that deepen the faithful's relationship with God. By reflecting on the life of Christ and the intercession of the Blessed Virgin Mary, devotions help Catholics to grow in faith, receive grace, and find comfort in times of trouble. Whether practiced individually or in community, devotions invite the faithful to experience God's love and mercy more profoundly, helping them to live out the Christian faith in their daily lives.

Adoration and Eucharistic Worship

At the heart of Catholic spirituality is the **Eucharist**, the Body and Blood of Christ. Catholic worship is centered around the **Eucharist**, as it is considered the source and summit of the Christian life. While the **Mass** is the central act of Eucharistic worship, there is another essential practice that Catholics hold dear: **Eucharistic Adoration**. Eucharistic Adoration is the act of reverently and prayerfully **adoring the Blessed Sacrament**—the consecrated host (bread) that Catholics believe becomes the **Body of Christ** during Mass.

Adoration of the Eucharist is a profound expression of **worship**, **gratitude**, and **intimacy** with God. It is a time set aside to gaze upon Christ's true presence in the Eucharist, reflect on His sacrifice, and offer Him praise, thanksgiving, and petitions. This form of devotion is particularly significant because it emphasizes the **real presence of Christ** in the Eucharist, offering a moment of silence and stillness to encounter God in a deeply personal and direct way.

In this chapter, we will explore the significance of **Eucharistic Adoration**, its practices, its role in personal spirituality, and the importance of reverence and awe in Eucharistic worship.

---

1. The Real Presence of Christ in the Eucharist

The foundation of **Eucharistic Adoration** lies in the Catholic belief in the **Real Presence** of Christ in the Eucharist. Catholics believe that during the **Mass**, when the priest says the words of consecration—**"This is My Body"** and **"This is My Blood"**—the bread and wine become the actual **Body** and **Blood of Christ**, although they retain the appearance of bread and wine. This transformation is called **transubstantiation**.

The doctrine of the Real Presence holds that Christ is truly present in the Eucharist—body, blood, soul, and divinity. This belief is rooted in Jesus' own words at the Last Supper, as recorded in the **Gospel of John** (6:51-58), when He states:

"I am the living bread that came down from heaven. If anyone eats of this bread, he will live forever; and the bread that I will give for the life of the world is my flesh."

In the Catholic faith, the Eucharist is not merely a symbol of Christ but His true **Body and Blood**, making it a **sacred reality** and the central point of Catholic worship. Adoration of the Eucharist is the response to this incredible gift—acknowledging Christ's presence and reverencing His offering of Himself for humanity's salvation.

---

2. Eucharistic Adoration: A Time of Worship and Reverence

What is Eucharistic Adoration?

Eucharistic Adoration is the practice of **adoring and worshiping** the **Blessed Sacrament** outside of the celebration of the Mass. During adoration, the consecrated host (the Body of Christ) is typically displayed in a **monstrance**—a vessel that allows the faithful to view the host. It may be placed on the altar in a church or chapel, where people can come and pray in silence, meditate on Christ's presence, and offer Him worship and adoration.

Eucharistic Adoration can take many forms:

- **Exposition of the Blessed Sacrament**: This is when the priest places the Eucharist in the monstrance, so it can be seen and adored by the faithful.

- **Silent Adoration**: During this time, the faithful can spend time in quiet prayer before the Blessed Sacrament, offering their hearts to God in adoration.

- **Benediction of the Blessed Sacrament**: At the end of a period of adoration, the priest blesses the congregation with the Eucharist in the monstrance.

Eucharistic Adoration is not simply an individual practice; it can also be done communally. In some places, Eucharistic Adoration is available **24/7**, where people come to spend an hour (often known as **Holy Hour**) in prayer and worship. This act of devotion can be incredibly profound, providing Catholics with a time to unite in prayer, reflect on Christ's sacrifice, and receive the graces He offers through the Eucharist.

---

3. The Spiritual Benefits of Eucharistic Adoration

Strengthening One's Relationship with Christ
Eucharistic Adoration is an opportunity to be in the **real presence of Christ** and to draw closer to Him. In adoration, Catholics open themselves up to Christ's love, mercy, and grace. As they sit in silence before the Eucharist, they encounter Christ in a deeply personal and intimate way. The silence allows individuals to listen more attentively to God, to reflect on His Word, and to experience His love and peace in their hearts.

Catholics believe that through this time spent with the Eucharist, they are **nourished spiritually**. Just as the body is nourished by food, the soul is nourished by Christ's presence. The Eucharist is a source of strength for those who are weary, comfort for those who mourn, and guidance for those who seek answers.

A Time of Reflection and Repentance
Adoration is also a time for **self-reflection** and **repentance**. In the stillness of prayer, the faithful can reflect on their lives, ask for God's forgiveness, and resolve to live more faithfully. Before the Eucharist, they can bring their burdens, sins, and struggles to Christ, trusting in His mercy and love. The Eucharist, as a sacrament of reconciliation, helps to heal wounds and provide peace for the soul.

Gratitude and Praise
In Eucharistic Adoration, Catholics express their **gratitude** for the gift of the Eucharist and Christ's ultimate sacrifice on the Cross. It is a time to thank God for His **unfathomable love** and to offer praise and worship for His presence in the Eucharist. Catholics are reminded of the

immense gift Christ gave to the Church by instituting the Eucharist at the Last Supper. By coming before the Eucharist, the faithful give honor to Christ and recognize His **self-giving love** for humanity.

---

4. The Power of Eucharistic Adoration in the Life of the Church

Adoration as a Source of Strength for the Church
Eucharistic Adoration is not only a personal devotion but also a communal act that strengthens the Church as a whole. The Catholic Church teaches that when the faithful gather in adoration before the Blessed Sacrament, they participate in a **universal** act of worship. The Eucharist is the bond that unites all members of the Church, and through adoration, Catholics are drawn into deeper **unity** with Christ and with each other.

Adoration also empowers the Church to carry out its mission. It provides the faithful with the spiritual resources needed to live out the teachings of Christ in the world. The graces received during Eucharistic Adoration equip believers to go out into the world and serve others, spreading the message of Christ's love and salvation.

Eucharistic Adoration as a Prayer for the World
Eucharistic Adoration is also a powerful prayer for the **world**. When the faithful spend time in adoration, they are interceding for the needs of the world—praying for peace, healing, justice, and the conversion of hearts. Many Catholics believe that their prayers during adoration have a profound impact, and they bring these petitions to Christ in the Eucharist, trusting in His power to bring about transformation in the world.

---

5. How to Participate in Eucharistic Adoration

For those interested in participating in Eucharistic Adoration, here are a few steps to guide your time of prayer:

1. **Arrive with Reverence**: Begin by entering the church or chapel quietly and respectfully. The presence of the Eucharist demands silence, and a respectful attitude is essential.

2. **Gaze Upon the Eucharist**: As you sit before the Blessed Sacrament, take time to gaze upon Christ in the Eucharist. Let your heart and mind focus solely on His presence.

3. **Pray**: During adoration, you may choose to pray spontaneously, or use prayers such as the **Rosary**, **litanies**, or **psalms**. Feel free to express your gratitude, offer your petitions, or simply rest in silence before Christ.

4. **Be Open to God's Grace**: Adoration is a time to receive from God. Be open to whatever He wants to offer you—whether it be peace, healing, strength, or insight.

5. **End with Benediction**: If the period of adoration includes Benediction, participate by offering a final prayer and receiving the blessing of the Eucharist.

Eucharistic Adoration is a profound practice that allows Catholics to engage deeply with the **Real Presence** of Christ in the Eucharist. It provides spiritual nourishment, strengthens the believer's relationship with Christ, and offers a time for personal reflection, repentance, and praise. Through adoration, the faithful not only honor the **sacrifice of Christ** but also bring the needs of the world to Him, trusting in His mercy and grace. Adoration is an invitation to enter into the intimate presence of God, to rest in His love, and to receive the strength needed to live out the Christian faith.

Chapter 5: Living the Catholic Life

The Call to Holiness: Growing in Virtue

The call to holiness is central to the Christian life. Every baptized person is called to be **holy**, to live a life reflecting the love and teachings of Jesus Christ. This call is not just for a select few but is the universal vocation of every member of the Church. Holiness is not an abstract ideal but a concrete journey, deeply intertwined with the process of **growth in virtue**. As Catholics, the goal is not just to follow a set of rules, but to become more like Christ—**loving, kind, humble, patient**, and ultimately, living a life of self-giving love.

Holiness is not something that we achieve on our own; it is the work of God's grace in us. However, the believer plays a crucial role in cooperating with God's grace by striving to cultivate **virtue**, which is the foundation of holy living. In this chapter, we will explore the nature of holiness, the role of virtue in the Christian life, and the practical ways Catholics are called to grow in virtue, especially through the **theological virtues** and the **cardinal virtues**.

---

1. What is Holiness?

Holiness Defined

Holiness is the **state of being consecrated to God**, living in a manner that is pleasing to Him and reflecting His nature. It means being set apart for God's purposes and striving to reflect His love, purity, and goodness in every aspect of life. Holiness is closely tied to **love**—the love of God and love of neighbor. Jesus summarized the whole law in two commands:

- **Love the Lord your God** with all your heart, soul, and mind (Matthew 22:37)

- **Love your neighbor as yourself** (Matthew 22:39)

The Catechism of the Catholic Church defines holiness as "the perfection of charity," which is living in perfect union with God and others, marked by self-giving love. Holiness does not mean perfection in the sense of never making mistakes, but rather it is a constant striving to **grow in love** and to be shaped into the image of Christ.

The Universal Call to Holiness
Holiness is not a special vocation for a select group of people, such as priests or religious. Rather, it is a universal call for all Christians, regardless of state in life. Every person is invited to live out their holiness in the unique circumstances of their life—whether as a student, teacher, parent, worker, or in any other role. The Second Vatican Council emphasized that all the baptized are called to holiness:
"All the faithful are called to the fullness of the Christian life and to the perfection of charity." (Lumen Gentium, 40)

Each person's journey to holiness will look different, but all are united in the goal of becoming more like Christ. Through holiness, Catholics are called to bear witness to the Gospel in their families, workplaces, communities, and the world.

---

2. The Role of Virtue in Growing in Holiness

What is Virtue?
Virtue is the habitual disposition to do good, to act in ways that are morally good, and to live a life of righteousness. It is a **moral excellence** that shapes one's character and enables the individual to live in accordance with God's will. Virtue is not simply about doing good actions but about becoming a good person, one whose nature is transformed by God's grace.

In the Catholic tradition, there are two kinds of virtues: **theological virtues** and **cardinal virtues**. These virtues help us to grow in holiness, guiding our actions, thoughts, and desires to be aligned with God.

The Theological Virtues

The **theological virtues** are the foundation of the Christian moral life. They are called "theological" because they relate directly to God and are infused in the soul by God's grace at baptism. These virtues are **faith, hope, and charity (love)**:

- **Faith** is the virtue by which we believe in God and all that He has revealed. Faith is the foundation of our relationship with God, allowing us to trust in His promises and live according to His Word.

- **Hope** is the virtue that enables us to desire eternal life with God and trust that God will provide the grace needed to achieve this goal. It helps us to remain steadfast in faith, even amid difficulties and suffering, knowing that God's promises are sure.

- **Charity (Love)** is the greatest of the theological virtues, the virtue that perfects all other virtues. Charity enables us to love God above all things and to love others as ourselves. It is the selfless, sacrificial love that Christ exemplified through His life, death, and resurrection.

These three virtues shape the life of the Christian. Through **faith**, Catholics come to know and trust God; through **hope**, they remain anchored in God's promises, and through **charity**, they are empowered to love God and others with the same love that Christ has for them.

The Cardinal Virtues

The **cardinal virtues** are the virtues upon which all other human virtues hinge. They are called "cardinal" from the Latin word **cardo**, meaning "hinge," as these virtues are the fundamental virtues upon which a virtuous life is built. The four cardinal virtues are:

- **Prudence** is the virtue that enables us to judge correctly what is right and choose the right course of action in every situation. It is the ability to make wise decisions, guided by reason and moral principles. Prudence helps us to apply the knowledge of what is good in particular situations.

- **Justice** is the virtue by which we give each person their due, treating others with fairness, respect, and equity. It involves recognizing the inherent dignity of every human being and working toward the common good.

- **Fortitude** is the virtue that enables us to endure trials, hardships, and difficulties with courage and perseverance. It strengthens us to remain faithful to God and our moral convictions, even in the face of suffering.

- **Temperance** is the virtue that moderates our desires and pleasures, ensuring that we do not give in to excess or selfishness. It is about finding balance and self-control in our emotions and actions, living in moderation rather than indulgence.

These cardinal virtues guide the believer in living out the theological virtues and cultivating a Christ-like character. They provide the foundation for moral actions that reflect God's will and love.

---

3. Growing in Virtue: Practical Steps

The process of growing in virtue is lifelong and involves **cooperating with God's grace**. Here are some practical ways to grow in virtue:

1. Prayer and Sacraments

A life of prayer is essential for growing in virtue. Through prayer, Catholics open their hearts to God and invite Him to transform their lives. Regular participation in the **Sacraments**—especially the **Eucharist** and **Confession**—strengthens the soul and helps the believer to grow in holiness. The Eucharist, in particular, is the source of **grace** and **strength** that empowers the Christian to live a virtuous life.

2. Study and Reflection on the Virtues

To grow in virtue, it is essential to **learn about the virtues** and reflect on how they apply to daily life. Catholics can read about the lives of saints, who exemplified virtues in extraordinary ways. Meditating on Scripture, especially passages that emphasize virtues, can also inspire growth in holiness.

3. Practice Self-Discipline

Virtue requires intentional effort and practice. Each day presents opportunities to practice the virtues of prudence, justice, fortitude, and temperance. Small actions—choosing to act justly, showing patience in moments of stress, or resisting temptations—help build virtuous habits. Over time, these habits become part of one's character.

4. Seek the Help of the Saints

The saints are models of virtue and holiness, and Catholics are encouraged to seek their **intercession** in the journey of growing in virtue. The saints show that it is possible to live a life of holiness, even in the midst of the challenges and struggles of human life. By praying to them and learning from their example, Catholics can draw closer to Christ.

---

4. Holiness in Daily Life

Holiness is not confined to moments of prayer or spiritual practices but must be lived out in every aspect of life. The call to holiness means striving to live a virtuous life in the midst of ordinary, everyday situations. Whether at work, school, or in family life, Catholics are called to reflect Christ's love through their actions, relationships, and choices.

Living a holy life means:

- **Loving others** through acts of kindness, compassion, and service.

- **Forgiving** those who hurt us, as Christ forgave us.
- **Pursuing justice** and standing up for the dignity of every person.
- **Being humble**, recognizing that all good things come from God.

The call to holiness is a call to live a life of **virtue**, following the example of Jesus Christ. By growing in the theological virtues of faith, hope, and charity, and cultivating the cardinal virtues of prudence, justice, fortitude, and temperance, Catholics are transformed into more faithful followers of Christ. This journey toward holiness requires prayer, self-discipline, reflection, and the grace of God, and it is lived out in the ordinary moments of daily life. As Christians grow in virtue, they become more deeply united with Christ and more effective witnesses of His love in the world.

Catholic Social Teaching: Faith in Action

Catholic Social Teaching (CST) is a rich body of doctrine that offers guidance on how Catholics are called to live their faith in the world, particularly in relation to social, economic, and political issues. Rooted in the teachings of Jesus Christ and the Bible, as well as in the Church's long tradition of social justice, CST is not just a set of abstract principles but a call to **action**—to transform society according to the values of the **Gospel**. It challenges Catholics to put their faith into practice, not just within the walls of the Church, but in the way they interact with and contribute to the world around them.

CST addresses a wide range of issues, including poverty, inequality, human dignity, care for creation, and the common good. It calls Catholics to respond to these challenges with love, compassion, and a commitment to justice. In this chapter, we will explore the key principles of Catholic Social Teaching, examine how they are rooted in the Gospel, and discuss how Catholics can live out these teachings in their daily lives as a way of practicing **faith in action**.

---

1. The Dignity of the Human Person

The first and foundational principle of Catholic Social Teaching is the **dignity of the human person**. This principle asserts that every human being, made in the image and likeness of God, has inherent dignity and worth. This dignity is not based on external characteristics such as race, nationality, gender, or social status, but on the **fact that all people are loved by God and have been given the gift of life**.

The **Catechism of the Catholic Church** teaches that human dignity is the foundation of all the Church's social teachings:
"The human person is and ought to be the principle, the subject, and the end of all social institutions." (CCC 1929)

Catholics are called to respect and protect the dignity of every person, especially those who are marginalized or oppressed. This means standing up for the rights of the poor, the unborn, the sick, the elderly, and all those whose dignity is threatened by injustice. As Jesus demonstrated through His ministry, **respecting human dignity** involves loving and caring for others, particularly the vulnerable, and promoting human flourishing.

Practical Application:

- **Advocate for human rights**: Support policies and initiatives that protect the dignity and rights of all individuals, especially the most vulnerable.
- **Stand against discrimination**: Combat racism, sexism, and other forms of prejudice that diminish human dignity.
- **Promote inclusivity**: Welcome and support those who are marginalized, such as immigrants, refugees, and the homeless.

---

2. The Common Good

The principle of the **common good** teaches that society should be organized in a way that promotes the well-being of all its members, especially the most vulnerable. It is the idea that the good of individuals cannot be separated from the good of the whole community. The common good requires that society's resources and institutions serve the **well-being of all**, not just the wealthy or powerful, but everyone, particularly those on the margins.

The **Compendium of the Social Doctrine of the Church** defines the common good as:
"The sum of those conditions of social life which allow social groups and their individual members relatively thorough and ready access to their own fulfillment." (Compendium, 164)

The common good involves ensuring that **economic, political, and social structures** serve human dignity, justice, peace, and the flourishing of all people. It calls Catholics to promote solidarity with one another and to pursue the well-being of society as a whole, not just their own personal interests.

Practical Application:

- **Support policies that serve the common good**: Advocate for economic and political policies that ensure access to education, healthcare, and employment for all.
- **Promote peace and justice**: Work for peace in communities and nations, striving to address the root causes of conflict and division.
- **Foster a culture of care**: In both personal and public life, encourage empathy and support for those in need, including the poor and the marginalized.

---

3. Solidarity

Solidarity is the virtue that highlights our **interconnectedness** as human beings, especially with those who are suffering or marginalized. It teaches that we are all responsible for one another, and that true peace and justice are only possible when people work together for the common good.

Solidarity involves recognizing that the suffering of one person affects us all. It challenges Catholics to put aside personal interests and stand in unity with others, especially the poor and oppressed, to address the issues that affect them.

The **Church's social teachings** on solidarity emphasize that this is not merely about charity or sympathy, but about **justice and advocacy**.

Catholics are called to actively work toward changing the systems that cause injustice and to promote the **dignity and rights** of all people.

Practical Application:

- **Work for social change**: Support efforts to address systemic injustices, including poverty, inequality, and discrimination.
- **Support social justice organizations**: Volunteer or donate to organizations that advocate for the poor, immigrants, or refugees.
- **Cultivate empathy**: In everyday life, make an effort to understand the struggles of others, particularly those who are disadvantaged or suffering.

---

4. Preferential Option for the Poor

One of the most distinctive and radical aspects of Catholic Social Teaching is the **preferential option for the poor**, which asserts that **the needs of the poor and vulnerable should be given priority in our actions**. This principle calls on Catholics to direct their resources, attention, and care toward those who are most in need, whether in their local communities or globally.

The preferential option for the poor is grounded in the teachings of Jesus, who consistently prioritized the needs of the poor, the sick, and the outcast. In the Gospel of Matthew, Jesus explicitly identifies Himself with the poor and the marginalized:
"Whatever you did for one of the least of these brothers and sisters of mine, you did for me." (Matthew 25:40)

By giving special attention to the poor, the Church seeks to restore justice and correct the imbalance created by economic, social, and political systems that often neglect or exploit the disadvantaged.

Practical Application:

- **Support the poor and marginalized**: Volunteer at shelters, donate to food banks, and support programs that provide services to the homeless and impoverished.
- **Advocate for fair wages**: Stand up for workers' rights, support policies that provide fair wages and working conditions, and fight for equal access to economic opportunities.
- **Examine personal spending habits**: Reflect on how personal consumption habits contribute to or alleviate poverty. Consider ethical consumerism, such as buying fair trade products.

---

5. Care for Creation

Catholic Social Teaching also includes a call to **stewardship** of the **environment**, grounded in the belief that creation is a gift from God and should be protected and respected. The **care for creation** is an essential part of Catholic faith because God created the world as a gift, and human beings are entrusted with the responsibility of caring for it.

Pope Francis' **encyclical Laudato Si'** underscores the need for an integral ecology, which integrates concern for the environment with concern for human beings, especially the poor and vulnerable who are most affected by environmental degradation. Catholics are called to be good stewards of the earth, protecting natural resources and promoting sustainability for future generations.

Practical Application:

- **Practice environmental stewardship**: Reduce waste, recycle, conserve water, and minimize energy consumption.
- **Support environmental justice**: Advocate for policies that protect natural resources and reduce the impact of pollution, especially in vulnerable communities.

- **Promote sustainable agriculture and fair trade**: Support farming practices that are environmentally sustainable and ethically sound.

---

6. The Role of Catholics in Society: Faith in Action

Catholic Social Teaching is not just a set of principles to be studied but a way of living the **Gospel** in the world. It calls Catholics to **active participation** in society—whether through **advocacy**, **service**, **education**, or **political action**—to transform the world in the image of Christ's love and justice. Faith is meant to be lived out in everyday life, not just in prayer and worship, but also in our actions toward others, especially those in need.

Catholics are called to **work for justice** in all areas of life—at home, in the workplace, and in the public square. This means being aware of issues like poverty, inequality, and environmental degradation, and actively working to address them. Through faith in action, Catholics can be instruments of God's love, helping to bring about **God's Kingdom on earth**.

Practical Application:

- **Engage in public life**: Vote for candidates and support policies that align with Catholic values of justice, peace, and human dignity.

- **Be a witness to Christ's love**: In daily interactions, live out the principles of CST, treating everyone with dignity, respect, and care.

- **Foster community**: Strengthen the bonds of charity and solidarity in your community through acts of service, outreach, and advocacy for the common good.

Catholic Social Teaching calls all believers to live out their faith in concrete ways, particularly through actions that promote justice, dignity, and the common good. It challenges Catholics to engage with the world, not just as passive bystanders, but as active participants in building a more just, compassionate, and sustainable society. By adhering to the principles of CST—such as the dignity of the human person, the common good, solidarity, and preferential option for the poor—Catholics are called to bring **faith into action**, transforming both themselves and the world around them in the light of Christ's love.

The Beatitudes and the Works of Mercy

The **Beatitudes** and the **Works of Mercy** are central teachings of the Catholic Church that provide a roadmap for living a life of holiness and compassion. Together, these teachings invite Catholics to live in imitation of Jesus Christ, who exemplified the values of humility, mercy, and love for others. The Beatitudes, found in **Matthew 5:3-12**, are a series of proclamations made by Jesus during the **Sermon on the Mount**, while the Works of Mercy, traditionally categorized into **corporal** and **spiritual** works, are practical actions that reflect the love and care we are called to show toward others.

In this chapter, we will explore the meaning of the Beatitudes and how they guide believers to live out their faith in the world. We will also examine how the **Works of Mercy** offer concrete ways to put the Beatitudes into action, helping Catholics grow in charity, justice, and mercy.

---

1. The Beatitudes: The Way to True Happiness

Understanding the Beatitudes

The Beatitudes are often referred to as the **"manifesto"** of the Christian life, outlining the attitudes and virtues that characterize those who are citizens of God's Kingdom. They turn conventional wisdom on its head by proclaiming blessings on those who are typically considered weak, poor, or suffering in this world. Rather than promoting success, wealth, or power, the Beatitudes call for the humility, meekness, and mercy that reflect the heart of God.

In his **Sermon on the Mount**, Jesus begins with the Beatitudes to reveal the values of God's Kingdom, contrasting them with the values of the world. The Beatitudes show us that **true happiness** and **blessedness** come not from material wealth or status but from living in alignment with God's will, especially through compassion, justice, and humility.

Here are the Beatitudes as found in **Matthew 5:3-12**:

- **Blessed are the poor in spirit, for theirs is the kingdom of heaven.**
    - This Beatitude invites us to **recognize our spiritual poverty** and need for God. It calls for humility and openness to God's grace, acknowledging that we can do nothing without His help.
- **Blessed are those who mourn, for they shall be comforted.**
    - Mourning here refers not only to grief over personal loss but also to sorrow over the suffering and injustices in the world. **God promises to comfort** those who suffer, whether through healing or through the solidarity of others.
- **Blessed are the meek, for they shall inherit the earth.**
    - Meekness is not weakness, but strength under control. It involves **gentleness and humility** in our relationships with others, rejecting arrogance and pride. **Meekness is a powerful virtue** that God rewards with lasting peace.
- **Blessed are those who hunger and thirst for righteousness, for they shall be filled.**
    - This Beatitude emphasizes the longing for **justice and righteousness** in the world. It reflects a deep desire to see God's will done on earth, and God promises to fulfill this desire by satisfying those who seek justice.
- **Blessed are the merciful, for they shall obtain mercy.**
    - Mercy is the heart of the Gospel message. **To be merciful** means to show compassion to those who are suffering or in need, offering forgiveness to those who wrong us. God promises that the merciful will receive His

mercy in return.

- **Blessed are the pure in heart, for they shall see God.**
    - Purity of heart involves **sincerity**, **honesty**, and **integrity**. A pure heart seeks God alone, free from the distractions of sin. Those who are pure in heart will have the privilege of seeing God face to face in the life to come.
- **Blessed are the peacemakers, for they shall be called children of God.**
    - Peacemakers work to reconcile relationships, resolve conflicts, and bring peace to the world. They reflect the **peace of Christ** and are called children of God because they imitate God's loving and reconciling nature.
- **Blessed are those who are persecuted for righteousness' sake, for theirs is the kingdom of heaven.**
    - Persecution for righteousness is a form of suffering that occurs when we stand up for **truth** and **justice** in the face of opposition. Jesus promises that those who suffer for His sake will be rewarded in heaven.

---

2. The Works of Mercy: Living Out the Beatitudes

The **Works of Mercy** are the concrete ways in which Catholics are called to live out the Beatitudes and embody the love of Christ in the world. The **Corporal Works of Mercy** focus on meeting the physical needs of others, while the **Spiritual Works of Mercy** address the needs of the soul. Both sets of works provide practical ways for believers to act with love, mercy, and justice in their everyday lives.

The Corporal Works of Mercy

The **Corporal Works of Mercy** are actions that care for the **bodily needs** of others. They involve the physical expression of love and compassion for those who are suffering, hungry, or in need. These works remind Catholics that love must be expressed in tangible ways.

1. **Feed the hungry**
   - Jesus taught that **feeding the hungry** is a direct way to serve Him (Matthew 25:35). This includes providing for those who lack sufficient food and working to address the systemic causes of hunger.
2. **Give drink to the thirsty**
   - Just as physical thirst is a basic need, so too is spiritual thirst. Offering water to the thirsty means providing for those in need, whether through charity or by advocating for access to clean water in impoverished communities.
3. **Clothe the naked**
   - Providing clothing to those who are without is a way of addressing **basic human dignity**. This work encourages us to consider the needs of the poor and make sure they have the essentials for survival.
4. **Shelter the homeless**
   - Catholics are called to offer hospitality and provide a safe home for those without shelter. This can include helping those who are living on the streets or offering a place for refugees and migrants.
5. **Visit the sick**
   - **Visiting the sick** is an act of mercy that shows love, solidarity, and compassion. It is not only about offering physical care, but also emotional and spiritual support for

those who are suffering.

6. **Visit the imprisoned**

    - Prisoners are often marginalized by society, but Jesus calls us to **visit** and support them, offering hope and compassion. This work also includes advocating for just and humane treatment of prisoners.

7. **Bury the dead**

    - The **dignity of the deceased** must be respected through proper burial. This work of mercy honors the memory of those who have passed and provides comfort to the grieving families.

The Spiritual Works of Mercy

The **Spiritual Works of Mercy** are acts that care for the **spiritual needs** of others. They involve guiding others in their faith, offering wisdom, comfort, and support, and helping others grow in holiness.

1. **Admonish the sinner**

    - Gently correcting those who are living in sin is a way of showing love and helping others find their way back to God. It requires humility, compassion, and wisdom.

2. **Instruct the ignorant**

    - Teaching the faith to others is a fundamental way of spreading the Gospel. Whether through formal instruction or informal conversations, Catholics are called to share the truths of the faith with those who do not know or understand them.

3. **Counsel the doubtful**

- Offering counsel to those who are uncertain or struggling in their faith provides comfort and guidance. This work encourages believers to offer a listening ear and help others find answers to their questions.

4. **Comfort the sorrowful**

   - **Comforting those who mourn** is a key expression of mercy. Whether through prayer, presence, or words of encouragement, Catholics are called to offer hope to those who are grieving.

5. **Bear wrongs patiently**

   - This work of mercy calls for patience in the face of injury or offense. Rather than retaliating, Catholics are called to forgive and bear suffering with grace, following the example of Christ.

6. **Forgive all injuries**

   - Forgiveness is at the heart of the Christian faith. Catholics are called to forgive those who have wronged them, just as God forgives their sins. This work is essential for healing relationships and promoting peace.

7. **Pray for the living and the dead**

   - Prayer is a powerful act of mercy. Catholics are encouraged to pray for the needs of others—whether they are still alive or have passed. Prayer for the souls of the deceased is an important part of the Church's tradition of caring for the departed.

3. The Connection Between the Beatitudes and the Works of Mercy

The **Beatitudes** and the **Works of Mercy** are interconnected. The Beatitudes describe the attitudes that Christians should cultivate in their hearts—humility, mercy, meekness, and a longing for righteousness—while the Works of Mercy are the practical outpourings of these attitudes in the world. For example:

- The **merciful** (Beatitude 5) are called to **show mercy** through the Works of Mercy, such as **forgiving the sinner** or **comforting the sorrowful**.
- Those who **hunger and thirst for righteousness** (Beatitude 4) will actively **work for justice** through the Works of Mercy, including **feeding the hungry** and **visiting the imprisoned**.

By living the Beatitudes, Catholics become more attuned to the needs of others, and through the Works of Mercy, they put their faith into action, demonstrating God's love and justice in the world.

The **Beatitudes** and the **Works of Mercy** provide a complete guide for living out the Christian faith. The Beatitudes outline the inner disposition of a Christian heart, while the Works of Mercy show how that disposition is expressed in the world. By living both, Catholics can fulfill Jesus' call to be His disciples, serving others with love, humility, and mercy. Through these teachings, Christians grow in holiness, transforming both their hearts and the world around them, one act of mercy at a time.

Fasting, Almsgiving, and Prayer: The Lenten Practices

The season of **Lent** is a time of **penance, reflection**, and spiritual renewal for Catholics. It marks the 40-day period leading up to **Easter**, mirroring the 40 days that Jesus spent fasting and praying in the desert before beginning His public ministry. Traditionally, **Lent** is an opportunity for Catholics to grow closer to God by engaging in practices of **self-denial**, **self-reflection**, and **acts of charity**. The three key practices of **fasting**, **almsgiving**, and **prayer** are foundational to the Lenten journey, and they help believers to purify their hearts, detach from worldly distractions, and focus on the deeper aspects of faith.

These practices are not just about giving up material things or performing outward acts of piety, but they are intended to help the faithful draw nearer to God and strengthen their relationship with Him. In this chapter, we will explore the significance of these three Lenten practices—**fasting**, **almsgiving**, and **prayer**—and reflect on how they help Catholics grow in holiness and become more attuned to the needs of others during this sacred time.

---

1. Fasting: The Discipline of Self-Denial

Understanding Fasting

Fasting is a spiritual discipline that involves abstaining from certain foods, activities, or comforts for a period of time. In the Catholic tradition, **fasting** is particularly observed during Lent as a way of **purifying the body and soul**, allowing the believer to detach from material things and focus on the spiritual life.

Fasting serves as an expression of **penance** and **humility**, as it involves denying oneself in order to grow closer to God. By fasting, Catholics are called to recognize their dependence on God for everything, and to remember that the things of this world—such as food and material comforts—are temporary. The practice of fasting helps believers to grow in **self-control**, develop a sense of **gratitude**, and cultivate **solidarity** with those who suffer from hunger and poverty.

Fasting during Lent is not simply about abstaining from food or drink but about making a deeper connection to God and intentionally redirecting one's heart toward Him. Jesus Himself fasted during His time in the desert and taught His followers the importance of this practice. In **Matthew 6:16-18**, He instructs His disciples:
"When you fast, do not look somber as the hypocrites do, for they disfigure their faces to show men they are fasting. Truly I tell you, they have received their reward. But when you fast, anoint your head and wash your face, so that your fasting will not be obvious to men, but only to your Father, who is unseen; and your Father, who sees what is done in secret, will reward you."

Purpose of Fasting
Fasting serves multiple purposes during Lent:

- **Purification**: Fasting helps cleanse the soul from sin and excess, encouraging believers to turn away from distractions and focus on God.

- **Solidarity with the poor**: By fasting, Catholics are reminded of those who suffer from hunger and poverty every day, prompting a desire to **share with others**.

- **Spiritual growth**: Fasting allows the believer to develop greater **self-discipline** and **detachment** from material things, freeing them to focus more on prayer and service to others.

Practical Aspects of Fasting

- **Abstinence**: The Church traditionally asks Catholics to abstain from eating **meat** on Fridays during Lent and to limit their intake of food on Ash Wednesday and Good Friday.

- **Fasting from other comforts**: In addition to food, Catholics may choose to fast from other comforts such as entertainment, social media, or luxuries, to help cultivate a spirit of **detachment** and spiritual focus.

- **Intentionality**: The key to fasting is not just abstaining from food but doing so with a sense of **purpose**—to grow spiritually, to purify the soul, and to align one's heart with God's will.

---

2. Almsgiving: A Call to Charity and Justice

Understanding Almsgiving
Almsgiving refers to the practice of **giving to those in need**, whether in the form of money, food, clothing, or other resources. It is an expression of **charity**, one of the theological virtues, and is integral to the Lenten journey. The Church teaches that almsgiving is a way of **loving our neighbor** and serving God, as Jesus Himself emphasized the importance of caring for the poor and marginalized.

In **Matthew 25:35-40**, Jesus identifies Himself with the poor and tells His followers that by helping those in need, they are directly serving Him:
"For I was hungry and you gave me something to eat, I was thirsty and you gave me something to drink, I was a stranger and you invited me in, I needed clothes and you clothed me, I was sick and you looked after me, I was in prison and you came to visit me."
This passage underscores the importance of **service to the poor** as an expression of love for God. Almsgiving during Lent is a call to share not only material resources but also our time, talent, and energy with those in need.

The Role of Almsgiving in Lent
Almsgiving is closely connected to the other Lenten practices of fasting and prayer. Through fasting, Catholics develop a spirit of **self-denial**, and through almsgiving, they direct the resources they save toward those in need. Almsgiving is not just a financial act but can also include **acts of service**, such as volunteering, helping the elderly, or supporting community initiatives aimed at uplifting the poor.

Almsgiving also helps **purify the heart** from selfishness and greed, reminding Catholics that **true wealth** is found in giving, not in accumulating. It helps the believer grow in **compassion**, **solidarity**, and **justice**—values that reflect the heart of Christ's ministry.

Practical Aspects of Almsgiving

- **Financial contributions**: Catholics are encouraged to donate to charitable causes, particularly those that serve the poor and marginalized, such as food banks, shelters, or aid organizations.

- **Volunteering**: Giving of one's time and skills to help others, such as visiting the sick, serving at a soup kitchen, or tutoring children, is also an important form of almsgiving.

- **Acts of kindness**: Small, everyday acts of charity—helping a neighbor, offering a kind word, or sharing resources—are ways to embody the spirit of almsgiving during Lent.

---

3. Prayer: Deepening the Relationship with God

The Role of Prayer in Lent
Prayer is the foundation of the Lenten journey. During Lent, Catholics are called to **renew** and **deepen** their prayer life, spending more time in communion with God through **personal prayer**, **liturgical prayer**, and **meditative practices**. Prayer is a powerful tool for spiritual growth, allowing the believer to grow in intimacy with God, seek His guidance, and receive the grace to live out the other Lenten practices.

Jesus modeled a life of prayer, often withdrawing to pray in solitude. He also taught His disciples how to pray through the **Lord's Prayer** and emphasized the importance of **persistent prayer** and seeking God's will. In **Matthew 6:6**, Jesus instructs:
"But when you pray, go into your room, close the door and pray to your Father, who is unseen; and your Father, who sees what is done in secret, will reward you."

Prayer as Communication with God
Prayer is more than just asking for things; it is about **building a relationship** with God, expressing love, gratitude, and reverence. During Lent, Catholics are encouraged to spend more time in **silent prayer**, **meditation**, and **reflection**, allowing God's presence to transform their hearts.

Practical Aspects of Prayer

- **Personal prayer**: Engaging in **quiet, personal prayer** every day, such as the Rosary, the Divine Mercy Chaplet, or spontaneous conversation with God, is an essential part of Lent.

- **Scripture reading**: The Lenten season provides an opportunity for **meditating on Scripture**, especially the **Gospels**, to deepen one's understanding of Jesus' life and teachings.

- **Attending Mass**: Catholics are encouraged to attend daily Mass during Lent, participating in the **Eucharist** and reflecting on the mystery of Christ's Passion, Death, and Resurrection.

- **Fasting and prayer**: Combining fasting with prayer intensifies the spiritual impact of these practices, helping to purify the heart and focus on God.

---

4. The Three Practices in Unity

Fasting, almsgiving, and prayer are all interconnected and should be practiced together in harmony during Lent. Each of these practices supports and strengthens the others:

- **Fasting** helps to focus the mind and body on God, while also creating space to be more generous in almsgiving.

- **Almsgiving** helps the believer to practice charity and justice, putting into action the humility learned through fasting and the reflection nurtured by prayer.

- **Prayer** is the foundation of the Lenten journey, helping Catholics to stay connected to God and to be transformed by His grace as they fast and give alms.

Together, these practices help Catholics to grow in **self-discipline**, **compassion**, and **love for God and neighbor**. They are not ends in themselves but means to help the believer become more fully united with Christ, who Himself fasted, prayed, and served others during His time on earth.

Fasting, almsgiving, and prayer are powerful practices that help Catholics to grow in holiness during Lent. They call us to be more intentional in our faith, to detach from worldly distractions, and to focus on the deeper aspects of life—God, others, and our eternal destiny. By embracing these practices, Catholics open their hearts to God's transformative love, allowing Him to purify their souls, strengthen their relationship with Him, and inspire them to live a life of greater service, compassion, and justice.

Chapter 6: The Catholic Church Today

The Role of the Pope and Bishops

In the Catholic Church, the Pope and the bishops play a central and vital role in guiding the faithful and leading the Church as a whole. Their authority is rooted in the teaching and mandate given by Jesus Christ to His Apostles, and especially to Peter, whom Catholics believe was made the first Pope. Together with the Pope, bishops form the hierarchy of the Church, responsible for maintaining **unity**, **faith**, and **doctrine** within the Catholic community. They ensure that the Church's teachings are faithfully transmitted and lived out in the world, offering pastoral care and leadership in accordance with Christ's mission.

In this chapter, we will explore the roles of the **Pope** and the **bishops**, their responsibilities in leading the Church, and how they exercise their authority in guiding the faithful to live according to the Gospel.

---

1. The Pope: The Vicar of Christ on Earth

Understanding the Role of the Pope

The **Pope** is the spiritual leader of the Catholic Church, regarded as the **Vicar of Christ**—a representative of Jesus on earth. His role is to **preside over the Church**, ensuring that its teachings remain faithful to the doctrine of Christ and guiding the Church in matters of faith, morals, and governance. The Pope is also considered the **successor of Saint Peter**, whose authority was given to him by Jesus when He said:
"You are Peter, and on this rock, I will build my Church, and the gates of hell shall not prevail against it." (Matthew 16:18)

This statement from Jesus marks the beginning of **papal authority**. Catholics believe that the Pope, as the bishop of Rome, holds a unique and divinely instituted position in the Church's governance. He is not only a figurehead but an active leader with a primary responsibility for safeguarding the unity and teachings of the Church worldwide.

Papal Infallibility

One of the most distinctive doctrines about the Pope is the teaching of

papal infallibility, which was formally defined during the First Vatican Council (1869-1870). This doctrine holds that when the Pope, in his official capacity as the **Supreme Pontiff**, makes a **definitive declaration on matters of faith and morals**, he is protected from error by the Holy Spirit. This guarantee, however, is not a blanket infallibility but applies only to **ex cathedra** (from the Chair of Peter) statements made under specific conditions. The doctrine of infallibility ensures that the Pope can preserve the Church from doctrinal error in crucial matters of faith.

Responsibilities of the Pope

- **Teaching and Upholding Doctrine**: The Pope's primary responsibility is to **preserve and teach the truths of the Catholic faith**. He is the final authority on matters of faith and morals, and he provides direction for the Church in dealing with contemporary issues.

- **Pastoral Leadership**: The Pope acts as the **shepherd** of the global Catholic community. He offers guidance, encouragement, and support to the faithful, addressing their spiritual needs and promoting the common good.

- **Unity of the Church**: The Pope's role is to preserve the unity of the Church. As the supreme pontiff, the Pope is seen as a symbol of **unity** for the universal Church, with authority over all bishops and dioceses. He ensures that the entire Church remains united in doctrine and purpose.

- **Global Influence**: The Pope is not only the leader of the Catholic Church but also an influential figure in the world. Through diplomatic engagement, humanitarian efforts, and interfaith dialogue, the Pope seeks to influence global peace and justice. The Holy See maintains **diplomatic relations** with over 180 countries, and the Pope often acts as a moral voice on issues such as poverty, war, climate change, and human rights.

2. The Bishops: Successors of the Apostles

Understanding the Role of Bishops

Bishops are the leaders of individual dioceses, or local churches, and are regarded as the **successors to the Apostles**. The word **bishop** comes from the Greek word *episkopos*, meaning **overseer** or **guardian**. Just as the apostles were entrusted by Christ with the mission of spreading the Gospel, bishops today carry on that mission in their respective dioceses.

Bishops share in the authority of the Pope but also have a distinct role within their dioceses. They are entrusted with the pastoral care of their local communities and are responsible for safeguarding **the faith**, **celebrating the sacraments**, and promoting the **spiritual welfare** of their people. As spiritual leaders, bishops are called to lead their dioceses with integrity, wisdom, and compassion.

Episcopal Authority and Collegiality

While the Pope holds supreme authority over the entire Church, bishops share in this authority in a **collegial** manner. This means that bishops, in union with the Pope, work together to ensure the **unity** and **apostolic faith** of the Church. They **collectively exercise authority** at the level of **ecumenical councils** and **synods**, which address important matters of faith, discipline, and pastoral concerns.

The bishops' role is not one of individual sovereignty but rather one of **shared responsibility** within the larger body of the Church. In their dioceses, bishops are responsible for **teaching**, **sanctifying**, and **governing** the faithful, while always remaining in union with the Pope.

Responsibilities of the Bishops

- **Teaching and Preaching**: Bishops are responsible for **teaching the faith** in their dioceses. They guide their clergy and faithful in matters of doctrine and ensure that the teachings of the Church are faithfully transmitted. Bishops also preach regularly, delivering homilies that help guide the faithful in their spiritual journey.

- **Sacramental Ministry**: Bishops have the responsibility to **administer the sacraments**, especially the **Sacrament of Confirmation**, which they alone can administer within their diocese. They also ensure that priests are properly trained to offer the other sacraments, particularly the **Eucharist** and **Reconciliation**.

- **Governance**: Bishops oversee the **administration** of the diocesan Church. They manage the finances, personnel, and overall structure of the diocese, ensuring that it operates in a way that supports the spiritual mission of the Church. Bishops are also responsible for **appointing priests** and deacons, ensuring they are properly trained and ordained to serve the people of God.

- **Pastoral Care**: One of the most important responsibilities of a bishop is to provide **pastoral care** for the people of his diocese. This involves **visiting parishes**, listening to the concerns of the faithful, and providing spiritual guidance and support. Bishops also need to be present at times of crisis, such as illness, death, or social upheaval.

- **Unity and Leadership**: While bishops have authority in their dioceses, they must always act in union with the **Pope** and the **universal Church**. They participate in the broader decision-making processes of the Church, including **synods** and **councils**, to help guide the direction of the Church and its response to modern issues.

---

3. The Pope and Bishops in Unity: The Apostolic Mission

The Pope and bishops work in unity to preserve the **apostolic mission** of the Church. While the Pope is the visible head of the universal Church, the bishops are **co-workers** with the Pope in spreading the Gospel and shepherding the faithful. This relationship is grounded in the belief that the Church is built upon the Apostles, and through the succession of the bishops, the Church maintains its apostolic nature.

In **Lumen Gentium**, the Vatican II document on the Church, the bishops are described as "**successors of the apostles**, who… have been made partakers of Christ's mission." Together with the Pope, bishops form the **magisterium** of the Church, which is the **teaching authority** that ensures the fidelity of the Church's doctrines.

The unity between the Pope and the bishops is not just one of authority but also of **collaboration** in the pastoral mission of the Church. They work together to address global issues, promote the Church's social teachings, and guide the faithful in living a life of holiness.

---

4. The Pope's Relationship with the Bishops

The Pope holds a unique role in maintaining the **unity** and **doctrine** of the Church, but he does not act alone. Bishops have significant roles in leading their dioceses and representing the Church in their respective regions. The Pope's relationship with the bishops is one of **spiritual fatherhood** and **guidance**, calling bishops to maintain the **unity of the faith** while respecting the unique pastoral needs of each local Church.

The Pope also works closely with bishops through mechanisms such as **ecumenical councils**, **synods of bishops**, and **papal visits**, which allow for regular collaboration and the sharing of insights regarding the needs of the Church.

The roles of the Pope and the bishops are foundational to the life and mission of the Catholic Church. The Pope, as the **Vicar of Christ**, leads the universal Church, safeguarding its unity and fidelity to the Gospel. The bishops, as **successors of the Apostles**, shepherd their dioceses, offering teaching, governance, and pastoral care to the faithful. Together, the Pope and the bishops work in harmony, with the Pope as the central figure of unity, ensuring that the Church remains faithful to Christ's mission and continues to be a beacon of truth, love, and justice in the world.

Catholicism in the Modern World

Catholicism, with over a billion followers worldwide, is a faith that has endured for over two millennia. Throughout its history, the Church has faced countless challenges, from internal divisions to external persecutions. However, it has always adapted to the changing times while maintaining its core beliefs. Today, the Catholic Church finds itself in a rapidly changing world, where global challenges—such as secularism, technological advancements, and social injustice—present both threats and opportunities.

In this chapter, we will explore how Catholicism interacts with the modern world, considering the Church's response to contemporary challenges, its role in the **global society**, its relationship with other religions, and how it addresses the needs of modern humanity. We will examine how the Catholic Church upholds its **timeless truths** while engaging with new ideas, social movements, and global issues.

---

1. Catholicism and Secularism

The Rise of Secularism

Secularism, the movement that advocates for the separation of religion from government and public life, has grown significantly in the modern world. In many countries, particularly in the West, secularism has led to a decline in religious participation, especially within traditionally Christian societies. The Catholic Church, which has been central to the life and culture of many nations for centuries, now faces the challenge of **religious indifference** or outright hostility in some parts of the world.

In **Europe** and **North America**, the rise of secularism has brought about a shift in societal values. Many people no longer see religion as necessary for personal or social development, and as a result, religious practice has diminished. **Catholics** in these areas may experience social pressure to conform to secular values that contradict Church teachings, especially in areas such as **moral ethics**, **marriage**, and **the sanctity of life**.

The Church's Response to Secularism
Despite the decline of religious influence in some regions, the Catholic Church remains **resilient** in its mission to evangelize and promote its teachings. The Church's response to secularism has been one of engagement rather than retreat. Through documents such as **Gaudium et Spes**, the Church has sought to speak to modern society on issues of **human dignity**, **freedom**, and **justice**, offering a vision of human life that transcends materialism.

The Church also advocates for the importance of **faith** in public life, asserting that **spiritual values** cannot be separated from **social** and **political issues**. It calls for a renewed recognition of the role of religion in shaping culture and guiding individuals toward **moral responsibility** and **ethical living**.

The Church's efforts to **re-evangelize** secularized societies include:

- **Strengthening Catholic education**: Catholic schools and universities remain key in transmitting the faith to the younger generation, fostering an understanding of Christian moral principles.

- **Cultural engagement**: The Church continues to promote its values through art, literature, and media, offering a counter-narrative to secular ideologies that diminish human dignity or ignore the spiritual dimension of life.

- **Public advocacy**: The Church actively participates in discussions on public issues, advocating for the **common good**, **human rights**, and **social justice**.

---

2. The Catholic Church and Technology

The Impact of Technology on Society
In today's rapidly advancing world, technology has radically reshaped **communication**, **commerce**, and even **human relationships**. The digital age, with its influence on **social media**, **artificial intelligence**, and **biotechnology**, has brought about new ethical and social challenges. Questions about privacy, digital addiction, and the moral implications of new technologies continue to emerge.

Catholicism has always valued the advancement of human knowledge, as it sees the pursuit of science as a way to better understand God's creation. However, technology also presents ethical concerns, particularly when it comes to issues such as **genetic engineering**, **bioethics**, **cloning**, and the **impact of technology on human relationships**.

The Church's Engagement with Technology
Pope **John Paul II**, **Pope Benedict XVI**, and **Pope Francis** have all addressed the implications of modern technology on human life and culture. In his encyclical **Fides et Ratio**, Pope John Paul II affirmed the compatibility of faith and reason, encouraging Catholics to engage with modern science and technology while upholding ethical principles grounded in faith.

Pope Francis, in his encyclical **Laudato Si'**, addressed the ethical responsibility of humans in relation to technological advancements, particularly as they impact the environment. The Church recognizes that **technology** must serve the common good, not exploit or harm creation, and that it must promote the **dignity of the human person**.

Catholics are called to navigate technological advancements with wisdom, ensuring that they do not undermine moral values or harm human flourishing. The Church encourages the ethical use of technology to promote **social justice**, **education**, and **sustainable development**.

---

3. The Catholic Church and Social Justice

The Church's Teachings on Social Justice
One of the defining characteristics of Catholicism in the modern world is its robust commitment to **social justice**. Rooted in the teachings of Jesus Christ and in the **Social Doctrine of the Church**, Catholic social teaching emphasizes the importance of **human dignity**, **solidarity**, and **the common good**. The Church believes that faith is not only a personal relationship with God but also involves active participation in the creation of a just and compassionate society.

Catholic social teaching addresses a wide range of issues, including poverty, inequality, human rights, labor rights, and care for the environment. Pope **Leo XIII**, in his encyclical **Rerum Novarum**, set the foundation for modern Catholic social thought by advocating for the rights of workers and the need for social and economic reform.

Key Principles of Catholic Social Teaching:

- **Dignity of the Human Person**: Every person is created in God's image and has inherent dignity and rights. This principle calls for the protection of the unborn, the elderly, the sick, and the marginalized.

- **Solidarity**: Catholics are called to stand with the poor and the oppressed, recognizing the interdependence of all people, particularly in a globalized world.

- **Preferential Option for the Poor**: The Church advocates for policies and actions that prioritize the needs of the poor and vulnerable.

- **Care for Creation**: The Church teaches that humans are stewards of God's creation and must protect the environment for future generations.

The Church's Role in Global Issues
Catholicism today is deeply involved in issues such as **poverty eradication**, **healthcare**, **human trafficking**, **refugee support**, and **environmental sustainability**. The Church's vast network of

organizations, including **Caritas**, **Catholic Relief Services**, and various religious orders, works to provide aid and advocate for justice on a global scale.

Catholics are called to **faith in action**, meaning that they are to live out their faith by engaging in efforts to heal broken relationships, end conflicts, and help build a more just and peaceful world. The Church's voice in global forums often calls for **compassionate action** and emphasizes the need to address the root causes of poverty and injustice.

---

4. Catholicism and Interfaith Dialogue

The Role of the Church in Interfaith Relations
As the world becomes more interconnected, the Catholic Church increasingly finds itself interacting with people of other faiths. Catholicism recognizes the **value of interfaith dialogue** as a means of promoting **peace**, **understanding**, and **mutual respect**. The Church believes that it can learn from the wisdom of other religious traditions while maintaining its own distinct faith in Jesus Christ.

The **Second Vatican Council**, in the document **Nostra Aetate**, emphasized the importance of dialogue with **Jews**, **Muslims**, **Hindus**, **Buddhists**, and other religious groups. It called for **respect** and **collaboration** in addressing common human concerns, such as poverty, war, and human rights.

Challenges and Opportunities
Interfaith dialogue is not without challenges, especially when it comes to theological differences or when religion is used to justify violence. However, the Church maintains that **peaceful dialogue** is crucial in a world marked by religious conflict and intolerance. Through dialogue, Catholics are called to witness to the **love of Christ** while building bridges with people of other faiths for the common good.

---

5. The Church's Response to Global Crises

Pope Francis and Global Leadership

Pope Francis has been a significant voice in addressing the moral and ethical dimensions of global crises. His papacy has been marked by a focus on issues such as **poverty**, **immigration**, **climate change**, and **economic inequality.** Through his encyclicals, particularly **Laudato Si'** and **Fratelli Tutti**, Pope Francis has called for a **global fraternity** and **solidarity** to tackle these issues.

In his papacy, Pope Francis has highlighted the importance of **human connection** and **compassion**, calling for action to address **global challenges** in a way that reflects Christ's teachings.

Catholicism in the modern world is a faith that is ever-evolving, responding to the challenges and opportunities presented by contemporary society. The Church remains steadfast in its commitment to **faith**, **justice**, and **human dignity**, even as it confronts secularism, technological advancements, and global injustices. By engaging with modern issues through the lens of the Gospel, the Catholic Church continues to play a vital role in shaping a world that reflects God's love, justice, and peace. Through **interfaith dialogue**, **social justice efforts**, and a renewed focus on **the common good**, the Catholic Church seeks to be a light in the modern world, guiding humanity toward a more compassionate and just future.

Ecumenism: Dialogue with Other Faiths

Ecumenism, derived from the Greek word *oikoumene* meaning "the whole world" or "the inhabited earth," refers to the movement within Christianity that seeks the **unity** of all Christians, overcoming denominational divisions and fostering greater understanding between different Christian traditions. However, ecumenism is not limited solely to intra-Christian dialogue. It extends to **interfaith dialogue**, where Catholicism, while remaining firm in its teachings, engages in respectful dialogue with adherents of other world religions.

In a pluralistic world where religious diversity is increasingly evident, the Church believes it has a responsibility to engage in **dialogue with other faiths**—whether through shared concerns about peace, justice, or social issues, or through a deeper understanding of each other's spiritual paths. In this chapter, we will explore the significance of **ecumenism** and **interfaith dialogue** within the Catholic Church, its theological foundations, the challenges it faces, and the positive outcomes that arise from such engagements.

---

1. Theological Foundations of Ecumenism in Catholicism

Christ's Prayer for Unity

Ecumenism finds its roots in the teachings of Jesus Christ, particularly His prayer for unity among His followers. In **John 17:21**, Jesus prays to the Father, saying:

"That they may all be one, just as You, Father, are in Me, and I in You, that they also may be in Us, so that the world may believe that You have sent Me."

This prayer underscores the profound importance of unity among Christians, as it is through unity that the Church can bear witness to Christ's presence in the world. Unity does not mean uniformity, but a shared commitment to the **core truths of the Christian faith**, particularly the life, death, and resurrection of Jesus Christ.

The Second Vatican Council and Ecumenism

The modern movement for Christian unity received a significant boost during the **Second Vatican Council** (1962–1965), a pivotal event in the life of the Catholic Church. One of the key documents to emerge from the Council was **Unitatis Redintegratio**, which focused on ecumenism. This document called for Catholics to engage in open and respectful dialogue with other Christian denominations to promote unity.

- The document acknowledged that **divisions** among Christians were a **scandal** and that all Christians should work together toward greater unity.

- It emphasized that unity should not be sought by erasing the distinctive identities of each tradition but through a **reconciliation of differences** and a **recommitment to shared values**.

Pope John Paul II and Ecumenism

Pope **John Paul II** took significant steps in furthering ecumenical dialogue, reaching out to Christian denominations, as well as to **Jews**, **Muslims**, and other religious communities. His famous declaration in **Ut Unum Sint** (1995) stressed the importance of working towards **visible unity** in the Church. He encouraged the faithful to be committed to unity in **truth** and **love**, and he emphasized that unity should reflect the **rich diversity** of Christian traditions.

Theological Challenges

The Church faces several theological challenges in ecumenical dialogue. While Catholics share much in common with other Christian groups, there are also significant theological differences, such as the **authority of the Pope**, **the role of the Virgin Mary**, and the **nature of the sacraments**. Despite these differences, the Church remains committed to dialogue and believes that the pursuit of unity should always be **faithful to the truth** of Christ.

---

2. The Church's Commitment to Interfaith Dialogue

While ecumenism focuses on fostering unity among Christians, **interfaith dialogue** seeks to build understanding, respect, and collaboration between Catholicism and other world religions. Catholicism's engagement in interfaith dialogue is motivated by the belief that all people are created in the **image of God** and deserve to be treated with dignity and respect, regardless of their religious background.

The Catholic Church's Approach to Interfaith Dialogue

The Catholic Church's teachings on interfaith dialogue are grounded in several principles:

- **Respect for the Religious Other**: The Church affirms the inherent dignity of every person and recognizes that **truths** about God can be found in many religious traditions. Catholicism acknowledges that **grains of truth** exist in the religions of the world, even though it remains firm in its belief that **Christ is the fullness of revelation**.

- **The Common Good**: The Church believes that interfaith dialogue is crucial in addressing **shared social issues** such as poverty, peace, human rights, and environmental sustainability. By coming together with people of other faiths, Catholics can work toward promoting the **common good** of all humanity.

- **The Freedom of Religion**: Catholicism holds that all people have the **right to religious freedom**, which means that individuals should be free to practice their religion without coercion or fear of persecution. Dialogue is conducted with the understanding that faith is a **personal gift** that must be freely embraced.

Nostra Aetate: The Church's Groundbreaking Declaration on Interfaith Dialogue

The document **Nostra Aetate**, issued by the Second Vatican Council in 1965, marked a significant step in the Catholic Church's approach to interfaith dialogue. It rejected the notion of **religious superiority** and called for **mutual respect** and **understanding** between Catholics and followers of other religions, particularly **Jews**, **Muslims**, **Hindus**, and **Buddhists**.

- For Jews, the Church rejected any form of **anti-Semitism** and acknowledged that **God's covenant with the Jewish people remains valid**.
- For Muslims, the Church affirmed the **shared belief** in the **one God** and acknowledged the importance of **Mary** and **Jesus** in the Muslim faith.
- For Hindus and Buddhists, the Church recognized the spiritual richness and wisdom of their traditions and called for dialogue in the spirit of peace and mutual respect.

---

3. The Role of Ecumenism and Interfaith Dialogue in Today's World

Promoting Peace and Social Justice

In an increasingly fragmented world, ecumenism and interfaith dialogue are essential for promoting **peace** and **social justice**. Religious differences have often led to **violence**, **conflict**, and **intolerance**. The Church believes that **dialogue** is a means to **bridge divides** and **build understanding** between different faith communities.

Pope **Francis**, in particular, has emphasized the importance of **interreligious dialogue** as a means of building bridges in a world plagued by **religious extremism** and **violence**. His outreach to **Muslim leaders**, particularly after his historic visit to the **United Arab Emirates** in 2019, demonstrates the Church's commitment to **peaceful coexistence** and working together on issues such as **refugee crises** and **climate change**.

Interfaith Dialogue as a Path to Understanding

Interfaith dialogue allows for mutual **learning** and **understanding**. Through these discussions, Catholics have the opportunity to learn from the spiritual practices, scriptures, and insights of other religions while deepening their own faith. For example, dialogue with Buddhists might focus on issues of **compassion** and **meditation**, while dialogue with Muslims often centers around shared beliefs about **God** and **morality**. Such encounters can enrich the spiritual lives of those involved, fostering deeper appreciation and respect for the diversity of God's creation.

The Challenge of Religious Pluralism

One of the challenges in interfaith dialogue is navigating the reality of **religious pluralism**—the coexistence of multiple religions in the same space. While the Church affirms the **universal nature** of Christ's salvation, it also acknowledges that people of other religions may be on their own unique spiritual journeys. Catholics are called to witness to their faith with humility, offering the message of Christ with respect and love, not as a means of coercion but as an invitation to share in the fullness of God's truth.

---

4. Practical Examples of Ecumenism and Interfaith Dialogue

Interreligious Prayer Services

In many parts of the world, Catholics participate in **joint prayer services** with other religious groups, particularly for global peace or in response to natural disasters. These services provide an opportunity to come together in **prayer** and **solidarity**, even while recognizing theological differences. Pope Francis' **World Day of Prayer for Peace** in **Assisi** is an example of such efforts, where leaders from different religions gather to pray for peace in the world.

Joint Social Initiatives

Catholic organizations frequently collaborate with other faith-based groups on issues like **poverty alleviation**, **healthcare**, and **refugee support**. For example, Catholic Relief Services often partners with Islamic, Jewish, and Protestant organizations to provide humanitarian aid in crisis situations. By working together, these groups witness to a **shared commitment** to **human dignity** and the **common good**.

Educational and Cultural Exchanges

Catholics also engage in **educational and cultural exchanges** with people from other religious traditions. These exchanges provide opportunities for individuals to learn about each other's beliefs, practices, and experiences, fostering mutual respect and understanding. Catholic universities and schools around the world offer courses on **interfaith relations** and regularly host interfaith events and dialogues.

Ecumenism and interfaith dialogue are essential to the Church's mission in the modern world. While remaining firm in the belief that **Christ is the fullness of revelation**, the Church is committed to engaging in **respectful dialogue** with other Christians and with followers of other faiths. This dialogue fosters peace, understanding, and collaboration on social issues, while also providing opportunities for spiritual enrichment. In a world marked by conflict and division, the Church continues to champion unity and cooperation, believing that through **dialogue** and **mutual respect**, humanity can work toward a more just and peaceful world.

Challenges and Controversies in the Church

The Catholic Church, with its over 2,000-year history, has been a beacon of faith, moral guidance, and community for billions of people across the world. However, like any large institution, it has faced significant challenges and controversies that have tested its strength, credibility, and mission. These challenges, often complex and multifaceted, arise from internal issues such as theological disagreements and scandals, as well as external pressures like secularism, cultural shifts, and political conflicts.

In this chapter, we will explore some of the major challenges and controversies the Catholic Church has faced, both historically and in the modern era. From internal divisions over doctrine and liturgy to scandals involving clergy abuse, we will discuss how the Church has navigated these difficult situations and how these events continue to shape its witness to the world.

---

1. The Sexual Abuse Crisis

The Scope and Impact of the Crisis
One of the most significant and damaging controversies in the modern Catholic Church has been the **sexual abuse crisis**. Beginning with revelations in the United States in the early 2000s, it soon became clear that sexual abuse by clergy was not an isolated issue but a widespread and systemic problem within the Church. Thousands of survivors have come forward to reveal the abuse they endured, and investigations have uncovered shocking patterns of **cover-up** and **mishandling** of abuse cases by Church authorities, including bishops and cardinals.

The crisis has caused immense harm to victims, shattered the trust of millions of Catholics, and damaged the Church's reputation globally. It has also raised critical questions about the Church's **accountability** and its handling of allegations of abuse within its ranks. The scandal has led to widespread calls for reform, transparency, and justice for the survivors, as well as a reevaluation of the Church's clerical culture.

The Church's Response

In response to the crisis, the Catholic Church has taken several steps, including:

- **Pope John Paul II** publicly acknowledging the scandal and expressing sorrow for the victims in the early 2000s.

- The **Charter for the Protection of Children and Young People**, established by the United States Conference of Catholic Bishops (USCCB) in 2002, outlined comprehensive guidelines for preventing abuse, reporting allegations, and holding perpetrators accountable.

- The **Dallas Charter**, which focused on holding bishops and other leaders accountable for failing to protect children, and implementing new protocols for **screening** and **training** clergy.

Despite these efforts, many critics argue that the Church's response has been slow and inadequate. Survivors and advocates continue to demand stronger measures, including the **laicization** (removal from the priesthood) of abusive clergy and the prosecution of individuals who have covered up abuse. Pope Francis, in particular, has sought to address the crisis head-on, calling for **zero tolerance** and greater transparency. The Vatican established the **Pontifical Commission for the Protection of Minors** in 2014 to help create better safeguarding policies worldwide.

Continued Challenges

While steps have been taken, the crisis is far from over. New allegations and reports continue to emerge, and the Church's credibility remains at stake. There is still significant **resistance** within some dioceses to full accountability, and many survivors continue to struggle with the Church's handling of their cases. As a result, the sexual abuse scandal remains one of the most difficult challenges facing the Catholic Church in the modern era.

2. Clerical Celibacy and the Vocation of the Priesthood

Debates Over Celibacy

The vow of **celibacy**, which requires priests to remain unmarried and abstain from sexual activity, has long been a distinctive aspect of Catholic priesthood. While many Catholics accept celibacy as a reflection of the priest's dedication to God and the Church, it has also been a subject of debate and controversy, particularly in modern times. Critics argue that mandatory celibacy may contribute to the **priest shortage**, especially in countries where the number of priests is declining.

Furthermore, celibacy has been criticized in light of the **sexual abuse crisis**; some argue that celibacy creates unhealthy psychological pressures, which might contribute to incidents of sexual misconduct. On the other hand, proponents of celibacy view it as a way to emulate the example of **Jesus Christ** and as a means of dedicating one's life entirely to God and the Church.

Calls for Reform

In recent years, there have been calls from within the Church to reconsider the requirement of celibacy, particularly in the context of **priestly vocations** in mission territories. Some argue that allowing married men to be ordained priests—especially in areas where there is a severe shortage of clergy—could help address the problem of insufficient pastoral care for Catholics. Pope **Francis** has hinted at being open to such reforms, especially in certain regions like the **Amazon**, where the number of priests is dramatically insufficient.

However, the debate on celibacy is highly sensitive, and there is considerable resistance from many within the Church, who see celibacy as an essential aspect of the priestly vocation. This issue continues to spark **intense debate** and remains a point of **contention** in the broader conversation about priesthood and Church reform.

3. Women in the Church: Roles and Leadership

The Question of Women's Ordination

The role of women in the Catholic Church has been a subject of significant debate and controversy, particularly regarding the issue of **women's ordination**. The Catholic Church teaches that only men can be ordained as priests, citing the example of **Jesus Christ**, who chose only male apostles. This teaching is rooted in the Church's tradition and its interpretation of Scripture.

However, there has been significant pressure, particularly from progressive Catholic groups and some feminist theologians, to allow women to be ordained as priests. Advocates argue that the exclusion of women from the priesthood is a form of **discrimination** and **inequality**, particularly in light of the many contributions women make to the Church in other capacities.

The Church's Response

The Vatican has firmly upheld the male-only priesthood, with **Pope John Paul II** stating in the **Apostolic Letter Ordinatio Sacerdotalis** (1994) that the Church does not have the authority to ordain women. This teaching has been reaffirmed by subsequent popes, including **Pope Benedict XVI** and **Pope Francis**.

While the Church maintains its position on ordination, there has been growing recognition of the importance of women in other roles within the Church, such as **lay leadership**, **teaching**, **evangelization**, and **social service**. Pope Francis has taken steps to include women more actively in decision-making roles, including appointing women to key positions in the Vatican's **governance** and **administration**.

Calls for Further Inclusion

Despite these advances, many continue to advocate for greater participation of women in the **governance** and **liturgical** life of the Church. Some hope that, over time, the Church may evolve in its approach to women's leadership, allowing for greater roles in the sacred life of the Church, even if not in the priesthood.

---

4. The Church and Political Engagement

The Church's Political Role
The Catholic Church has long been involved in political matters, advocating for issues related to **social justice**, **human rights**, and **moral values**. The Church has often spoken out on matters such as **poverty**, **war**, **immigration**, and **economic inequality**, calling on governments and political leaders to act in accordance with **Catholic social teaching**.

However, the Church's involvement in politics has sometimes led to controversy, especially when the Vatican or individual bishops speak out on **hot-button issues** such as **abortion**, **same-sex marriage**, and **euthanasia**. Critics argue that the Church's political engagement can be **too partisan** or **intrusive**, while others contend that the Church must be a voice for **moral clarity** in a world where secular ideologies often conflict with Christian values.

Political Divisions within the Church
Another challenge facing the Church is the **internal political division** among its clergy and laity. While the Vatican speaks with one voice on many issues, local bishops, priests, and Catholic laypeople may hold diverse political views. In countries like the United States, for example, political divisions often reflect differing opinions on **immigration**, **economic justice**, and **human life issues**, which can complicate the Church's ability to present a unified stance.

Pope Francis, in particular, has faced both support and criticism for his **political** and **social** teachings, especially his stance on **economic inequality** and **environmental justice**. His advocacy for **care for creation** through his encyclical **Laudato Si'** and his criticisms of **capitalism** have drawn both admiration and backlash from various political factions within the Church.

---

5. The Church and Secularism

The Rise of Secularism

As secularism continues to grow in influence, particularly in **Western countries**, the Catholic Church faces significant challenges in preserving its moral voice in public life. Secularism, which advocates for the separation of religion from state and public life, often clashes with the Church's teachings on matters like **family life**, **sexual ethics**, and **the sanctity of life**.

Catholicism's position on these issues is increasingly out of step with popular cultural values, particularly as issues like **same-sex marriage**, **abortion rights**, and **euthanasia** become more widely accepted in society. The **Church's stance** on these matters has led to tensions between religious freedom and governmental policies that favor secular, humanist values.

The Catholic Church continues to navigate a wide range of **internal and external challenges**, each of which plays a significant role in shaping its mission and witness in the modern world. While controversies such as the **sexual abuse crisis**, the role of **women** in the Church, **clerical celibacy**, and **political engagement** remain significant hurdles, the Church continues to adapt, calling for **renewed faithfulness**, **transparency**, and **commitment** to the Gospel message. Amid these difficulties, the Church remains focused on its core mission—**proclaiming Christ's love** and **working for the common good**—and its ongoing journey through these challenges will continue to define its role in the world for years to come.

Chapter 7: The Saints and Their Lives of Faith

The Catholic Church honors saints as models of holiness, virtue, and unwavering faith in God. Saints are men and women who, through their lives and actions, have exemplified the teachings of Christ, showing the world what it means to live as a true disciple. They come from all walks of life and from various time periods, yet they share a common devotion to God and a willingness to sacrifice everything for the sake of their faith.

In this chapter, we will explore the lives of several saints, examining their unique paths to holiness, their struggles, and the legacies they left behind. Through these stories, we will see how the saints' experiences reflect the beauty and challenge of living the Christian life, and how their examples can inspire and guide Catholics today.

---

1. The Path to Holiness: The Role of the Saints in Catholicism

What Does It Mean to Be a Saint?
In Catholic theology, **sainthood** is not about perfection, but rather about a person's **unwavering love for God** and **commitment to following Christ's example**. Saints are not necessarily flawless individuals but are people who, through God's grace, overcome their weaknesses and live lives of extraordinary virtue and faith.

The process of becoming a saint is known as **canonization**, which involves a thorough investigation into the person's life, virtues, and miracles attributed to their intercession. The Church believes that the saints are **models for the faithful** and intercessors who pray for us in heaven. Saints show us that sanctity is possible for everyone, regardless of their social status, talents, or circumstances. They embody the **universal call to holiness** that is present in every Christian's life.

The Role of Saints in Catholic Worship
Saints are revered and honored in the Catholic Church, but they are not worshipped. Catholics believe in **asking saints to intercede on their behalf** before God, much like one might ask a friend or family member to pray for them. The saints' **intercessory power** is believed to come from their closeness to God and the grace they received during their lives.

Saints are honored through feast days, prayers, and devotionals such as the **Litany of the Saints** and **the veneration of relics**. Churches dedicated to specific saints hold **celebrations** in their honor, and their **shrines** and **tombs** are often places of pilgrimage.

---

2. The Lives of the Saints: Exemplars of Faith

Saint Augustine of Hippo: A Life Transformed
Saint **Augustine** is one of the most influential saints in the history of the Church. Born in 354 in North Africa, Augustine initially lived a life marked by indulgence, pride, and rebellion. However, through the prayers of his mother, **Saint Monica**, and the preaching of **Saint Ambrose**, he experienced a profound conversion.

Augustine's writings, especially his **Confessions**, revealed his inner struggles and the overwhelming grace he received from God. He is known for his emphasis on the grace of God in the life of the believer and for his teachings on **original sin** and **the nature of the Church**. As a bishop, Augustine worked tirelessly to guide his flock, and his theological insights continue to shape Catholic thought to this day.

His story teaches us that no one is beyond God's grace and that a person can always turn their life around, no matter how far they may have strayed from God's path.

Saint Francis of Assisi: Embracing Poverty and Simplicity
Saint **Francis of Assisi** was born into a wealthy family in 1182, but he chose to renounce all material wealth and live a life of poverty and simplicity. He believed that true happiness could only be found in

complete detachment from earthly possessions and in living a life of service to others, particularly the poor and marginalized.

Francis's life of poverty, humility, and care for God's creation has had a profound influence on the Church and the world. He is often depicted with animals, symbolizing his love for creation, and he is known for establishing the **Franciscan Order**, which emphasizes simplicity, prayer, and a love for nature.

Saint Francis's story reminds us that true wealth is not found in material things but in **spiritual richness**, and that **God's love** can be experienced through a life of simplicity, service, and **joy in creation**.

Saint Therese of Lisieux: The Little Way of Love
Saint **Therese of Lisieux**, also known as the **Little Flower**, lived a short but impactful life. Born in 1873 in France, Therese entered the Carmelite convent at the age of 15 and spent her life in deep prayer and devotion. She became famous for her simplicity and her approach to holiness, which she called the **"Little Way"**.

Therese believed that even the smallest acts of love, performed with great love and for the glory of God, could lead to holiness. She emphasized that **greatness** in the spiritual life does not require extraordinary acts but can be achieved by faithfully doing everyday tasks with a loving heart. Her spirituality focuses on the **childlike trust** in God and the power of **small sacrifices** made with great love.

Her life encourages us to embrace **simplicity and humility**, reminding us that sanctity is found in everyday moments and that even small acts of love can have eternal significance.

---

3. The Saints as Intercessors

The Intercession of the Saints
Catholics believe in the power of the saints' **intercession**—the act of saints praying on behalf of individuals here on earth. Just as we ask friends and family to pray for us, Catholics believe that the saints, being close to God in heaven, can pray for us more effectively.

This intercession is particularly important when Catholics seek **God's grace** in times of need, such as for healing, guidance, or comfort. The saints are seen as examples of how to live holy lives, and they act as **spiritual advocates** for the faithful.

For example, **Saint Jude** is known as the patron saint of **hopeless cases**, and many turn to him when facing difficult situations. Similarly, **Saint Rita of Cascia** is invoked for **impossible causes**. These saints, along with countless others, offer hope and support through their intercession.

---

4. The Importance of Relics and Pilgrimages

Relics: Symbols of Holiness
A relic is a physical object or a part of the body of a saint that is venerated by the faithful. Relics are often considered a tangible connection to the **holiness** and **grace** of the saints, as they are believed to carry a portion of the saint's **spiritual power**.

There are three types of relics:

1. **First-class relics**: Direct parts of the saint's body (e.g., bones, hair).
2. **Second-class relics**: Objects the saint used, such as clothing or books.
3. **Third-class relics**: Items that have been touched to a first-class relic.

Relics are venerated in many Catholic churches, and pilgrims often visit these sites to ask for blessings and to deepen their connection to the saints.

Pilgrimages: Journeying to Holy Sites
Pilgrimages to the tombs of saints or places where saints lived and worked are an important part of Catholic devotion. **Rome**, **Lourdes**,

Santiago de Compostela, and **Assisi** are some of the most famous pilgrimage destinations for Catholics, as they are home to the relics of important saints.

Pilgrimages are opportunities for **spiritual renewal**, **penance**, and a deeper connection to the Church's history and the communion of saints. They allow Catholics to walk in the footsteps of the saints and draw inspiration from their example of faith.

---

5. Modern Saints: Living the Faith Today

Saint Mother Teresa of Calcutta
Saint **Mother Teresa**, known for her work with the poor and the sick in the slums of Calcutta, is a modern example of **selfless service** and compassion. She founded the **Missionaries of Charity** and dedicated her life to caring for the most destitute and marginalized people. Her love for the **poor**, her deep **spirituality**, and her unshakable faith in God led to her canonization as a saint in 2016.

Saint John Paul II
Pope **John Paul II**, one of the most beloved and influential popes in modern history, was canonized in 2014. His **papacy** was marked by his efforts to **renew the Church**, engage in interfaith dialogue, and promote peace and justice worldwide. His teachings on **human dignity**, the **sanctity of life**, and the **importance of family** continue to impact the Church today.

These modern saints show us that the call to holiness is not confined to the past but remains present in our everyday lives. Through their examples, we are reminded that sainthood is a journey of **faith, sacrifice, and service**, and that each of us is called to live out that faith in our own unique way.

The saints are a living testament to the power of **God's grace** at work in human lives. They show us that no matter how imperfect we are, holiness is possible if we strive to live according to God's will. Their examples inspire us to be courageous in faith, humble in service, and loving in all we do. The saints teach us that a life of **faith** is not just about following rules but about living a life of love, sacrifice, and devotion to God and others. Their intercession, their relics, and their stories continue to guide us toward our ultimate goal—union with God in heaven. Through the saints, we are reminded that the path to holiness is open to all who wish to walk it, and with **God's grace**, we can live lives worthy of sainthood.

Chapter 8: The Role of Mary and the Communion of Saints

Understanding Mary's Role in Catholic Faith

In Catholicism, **Mary, the Mother of Jesus**, holds a unique and profound place within the faith. Revered as the **Mother of the Church**, Mary's role transcends that of a simple historical figure; she is considered an eternal model of faith, humility, and devotion to God. Throughout centuries, Catholics have honored her not only as the mother of **Jesus Christ** but also as a powerful intercessor, a symbol of the Church's maternal love, and a **spiritual mother** to all believers.

In this chapter, we will explore Mary's role in Catholic theology and devotion, examining her **unique relationship with God**, her **participation in salvation history**, and how Catholics relate to her in **prayer** and **devotion**. We will also address some of the central doctrines associated with Mary, such as her **Immaculate Conception**, **Perpetual Virginity**, and **Assumption**, and how these beliefs shape Catholic spirituality.

---

1. Mary as the Mother of God

The Divine Motherhood of Mary
The Catholic Church believes that Mary, as the **Mother of Jesus**, is also the **Mother of God** (Theotokos, meaning "God-bearer"). This belief was solemnly declared at the **Council of Ephesus** in 431 AD, which affirmed that Jesus Christ is both fully **God** and fully **man**, and that Mary, as His mother, can rightly be called the **Mother of God**.

This title is not meant to elevate Mary above her son but to emphasize her **central role** in the divine plan of salvation. By consenting to God's will and accepting the divine calling to be the mother of the **Messiah**, Mary participated in God's plan for the redemption of humanity. Through her **fiat** (her "yes" to God's message from the angel Gabriel), Mary became an instrument through which God entered the world in human form.

Mary's motherhood is not limited to her physical role but extends to her spiritual motherhood over all Christians. As the **Mother of the Church**, she is seen as the protector and nurturer of the faithful, guiding them towards a deeper relationship with her Son, Jesus Christ.

---

2. The Immaculate Conception: Mary's Freedom from Sin

Understanding the Immaculate Conception
The doctrine of the **Immaculate Conception** is one of the most significant teachings in Catholicism regarding Mary. It holds that from the moment of her conception, Mary was preserved from original sin by the grace of God. This doctrine was formally declared by **Pope Pius IX** in 1854, emphasizing that Mary, in preparation for her unique role as the Mother of God, was conceived without the stain of sin.

The **Immaculate Conception** does not mean that Mary was divine or that she did not need a savior, but rather that she was **singularly preserved** from sin in order to be a fitting vessel to bear Christ. Catholics believe that this unique privilege is a result of God's grace, and it underscores Mary's **special holiness** and role in salvation history.

Mary's Immaculate Conception and the Incarnation
The **Immaculate Conception** is viewed as an important preparation for the **Incarnation** of Christ. By preserving Mary from original sin, God ensured that the vessel through which the **Word became flesh** was pure and without sin. This teaching deepens the Catholic understanding of the sanctity and mystery of Mary's role in God's salvific plan.

---

3. Mary's Perpetual Virginity

Mary's Ever-Virginity
One of the central doctrines about Mary in Catholicism is her **Perpetual Virginity**—the belief that Mary remained a virgin throughout her life, before, during, and after the birth of Jesus. The Catholic Church affirms that Jesus was born of a **virgin**, not only because this was a miraculous

sign of His divine nature but also because it is a reflection of Mary's **total devotion** to God and her complete submission to His will.

The belief in Mary's perpetual virginity is not merely a physical attribute but a symbol of her **spiritual purity** and her role as a **new Eve**. Just as Eve's disobedience led to sin entering the world, Mary's obedience to God, in her fiat, became the means by which salvation was brought into the world.

Symbolic Meaning of Mary's Virginity
The doctrine of **Perpetual Virginity** also carries symbolic significance. Mary's virginity represents her total **dedication** to God and **purity of heart**, qualities that Catholics are called to emulate in their own relationship with Christ. It reflects the Church's teaching that to be fully united with Christ, the faithful must also be open to God's will and remain spiritually **pure** in their relationship with Him.

---

4. The Assumption: Mary's Glorious End

Mary's Bodily Assumption into Heaven
Another important doctrine in Catholicism is the **Assumption of Mary**, which teaches that at the end of her earthly life, Mary was taken **body and soul** into heaven. This teaching was formally declared by **Pope Pius XII** in 1950, though it has been believed by Catholics for centuries.

The **Assumption** reflects Mary's unique role in salvation history and her special relationship with God. Just as Jesus ascended to heaven, so too, Mary, the Mother of God, was assumed into glory. The Assumption is seen as a sign of the **ultimate victory over death** and a promise to all believers that, through Christ, the faithful will be raised to eternal life.

The Assumption and Christian Hope
The belief in Mary's Assumption offers **hope** and **consolation** to Catholics, as it assures them that one day they too will experience the **resurrection of the body**. Mary's Assumption is a symbol of the ultimate **reward for the faithful**—eternal life with God. Catholics see it

as an affirmation that **God honors those who honor Him** and that a life devoted to God will be eternally rewarded.

---

5. Mary as the Intercessor and Advocate

Mary's Role as Intercessor

Catholics believe that Mary, as the **Mother of the Church**, has a special role in **interceding** for the faithful. She is seen as a loving mother who listens to the prayers of her children and presents them to her Son, Jesus. Catholics often pray to Mary asking for her intercession in various areas of their lives, trusting that she, being close to Christ, has a unique ability to advocate on their behalf.

The **Hail Mary** prayer, one of the most well-known Marian prayers, encapsulates this role of intercession. By invoking Mary's intercession, Catholics ask for her prayers and protection, trusting that her maternal love for them will lead them closer to Christ.

Mary's Intercession in Catholic Tradition

Throughout history, many Catholics have experienced the power of Mary's intercession in times of difficulty, illness, or danger. Pilgrimages to Marian shrines, such as those in **Lourdes, Fatima**, and **Guadalupe**, have been places of great devotion and miraculous healings. These stories reflect the belief that Mary, in her compassion, continues to watch over the faithful and bring them closer to God.

---

6. Devotion to Mary: Practices and Prayers

The Rosary: A Marian Prayer

The **Rosary** is one of the most popular forms of devotion to Mary in Catholicism. It is a prayer that reflects on the **life of Christ** through the eyes of His mother, Mary. The Rosary consists of a series of prayers, including the **Our Father**, **Hail Mary**, and **Glory Be**, while meditating on specific events in the life of Christ called **Mysteries**. The Rosary is a powerful tool for deepening one's spiritual life and growing closer to God through the intercession of Mary.

Other Marian Devotions
Other Marian devotions include the **Angelus** prayer, the **Salve Regina** (Hail Holy Queen), and the **Magnificat** (Mary's prayer of praise in the Gospel of Luke). These prayers and devotions help Catholics focus on Mary's virtues and her closeness to Christ, offering a way to grow in faith and humility.

---

7. Mary in Catholic Life and Liturgy

Feasts and Solemnities of Mary
Mary is honored throughout the liturgical year in the Catholic Church with special feast days and solemnities. Some of the major Marian feast days include:

- **The Immaculate Conception** (December 8)
- **The Assumption** (August 15)
- **The Annunciation** (March 25)
- **Our Lady of Guadalupe** (December 12)

These feast days celebrate key moments in Mary's life, such as her conception, her assumption into heaven, and her pivotal role in God's plan for salvation. Through these celebrations, Catholics deepen their relationship with Mary and draw closer to her Son, Jesus.

Mary holds a unique and essential place in Catholic theology and devotion. Her **motherhood**, **holiness**, and **intercessory role** make her a powerful figure for Catholics, guiding them closer to Christ through prayer, devotion, and reflection on her life. The doctrines that honor her, such as the **Immaculate Conception**, **Perpetual Virginity**, and

Assumption, underscore her special place in salvation history and her ongoing spiritual motherhood for all believers.

The Immaculate Conception and the Assumption

The doctrines of the **Immaculate Conception** and the **Assumption** are two of the most important and distinctive teachings of the Catholic Church regarding the Virgin Mary. These beliefs not only highlight Mary's unique role in salvation history but also emphasize the Church's understanding of holiness, grace, and the promise of eternal life. While both doctrines celebrate Mary's exceptional place in God's divine plan, they serve different theological purposes and hold profound significance for the life of the Church.

In this chapter, we will explore both the **Immaculate Conception** and the **Assumption**, examining their theological foundations, the historical development of these doctrines, and their impact on Catholic spirituality. We will also consider the significance of these teachings for the faithful today and how they deepen the Catholic understanding of the **relationship between grace, holiness, and salvation**.

---

1. The Immaculate Conception: Mary's Freedom from Sin

Understanding the Doctrine of the Immaculate Conception
The **Immaculate Conception** is the Catholic belief that **Mary was conceived without original sin**. Unlike every other human being, who inherits original sin from Adam and Eve, Mary was preserved from this stain from the moment of her conception, so that she could be a fitting vessel to bear the Son of God. This teaching was formally defined by **Pope Pius IX** in 1854, but it was held as part of Catholic tradition long before that.

The key point of this doctrine is that **Mary was conceived in a state of grace**, free from the taint of original sin. This unique grace was given to her by God in preparation for her role as the **Mother of Jesus**, the Savior of the world. Catholics believe that this grace did not arise from any merit on Mary's part, but was a **divine gift** freely given by God.

Theological Significance
The Immaculate Conception emphasizes **God's sovereignty** and **grace** in the process of salvation. It illustrates that God, in His infinite mercy, prepared a holy and pure vessel for the birth of Jesus. Mary's freedom from original sin enabled her to fully cooperate with God's plan of redemption, serving as a model of **purity, humility, and obedience**.

Theologically, the Immaculate Conception highlights the Church's belief in the **prevenient grace** of God—that is, God's grace that precedes and prepares the soul for holiness before any action on the part of the individual. Mary's sinlessness is not an attribute of her own power but a gift of God's grace, showing that **grace and holiness are central to the Christian life**.

Scriptural Basis
Though the doctrine was not explicitly stated in Scripture, Catholics point to passages that **suggest Mary's unique holiness**. For instance, in the **Annunciation** (Luke 1:28), the angel Gabriel greets Mary as **"full of grace"** (Greek: *kecharitomene*), a term that indicates a special favor bestowed upon her by God. The Church interprets this as an indication that Mary was filled with grace from the moment of her conception, which aligns with the teaching of the Immaculate Conception.

Additionally, the Church sees Mary as the **new Eve**, whose obedience and purity contrast with the disobedience and fall of the first Eve (Genesis 3). Just as Eve's disobedience brought sin into the world, Mary's purity and yes to God brought forth the Savior.

Impact on Catholic Devotion
The dogma of the **Immaculate Conception** invites Catholics to see Mary as the **paragon of grace** and a model for their own lives. She is the perfect **model of obedience** to God's will and the **ideal disciple**. The belief in her Immaculate Conception inspires Catholics to strive for holiness, knowing that God's grace can purify and transform even the most flawed and sinful human beings.

---

2. The Assumption: Mary's Glorious End

Understanding the Doctrine of the Assumption

The doctrine of the **Assumption** teaches that **Mary, at the end of her earthly life, was taken body and soul into heaven**. Unlike the death and burial of other saints, Mary was not subjected to the decay of the body after death. Instead, God preserved her from this final indignity, elevating her to heaven in the fullness of her humanity.

The dogma of the **Assumption** was formally defined by **Pope Pius XII** in 1950, but, like the Immaculate Conception, it was a belief held by the faithful long before its official proclamation. The Catholic Church teaches that Mary's Assumption is a sign of her **special relationship with God** and a promise to all Christians of the resurrection and eternal life.

Theological Significance

The **Assumption** underscores the **dignity** of the human body and the **ultimate victory over death**. It affirms the Catholic belief that the body, created by God, is not merely a temporal vessel but is destined for eternal life with God. The **Assumption** is a celebration of the **unity** of body and soul in the eternal presence of God.

Mary's Assumption is a **glorious confirmation** of the resurrection of the body, a core Christian belief that emphasizes that Christ's **victory over death** is meant for all believers, not just the soul. It offers hope to all Christians that one day, their bodies will be resurrected and reunited with their souls in the presence of God.

Scriptural Basis

While the Assumption is not explicitly mentioned in Scripture, Catholics see the teaching as a natural conclusion based on Mary's special place in salvation history. The **Book of Revelation** (12:1-2) describes a woman clothed with the sun, with the moon under her feet, and a crown of twelve stars on her head. This image is often interpreted as a symbol of Mary, whose **glorification** in heaven reflects her role as the **Mother of the Church**.

Furthermore, the Assumption is seen as the fulfillment of God's promise to Mary, as given in **Luke 1:48**, where Mary prophesies that from that moment on, **"all generations will call me blessed."** The Assumption is an extension of this blessing, showing that her role as the Mother of God has been rewarded with the ultimate honor—being taken into heaven.

Impact on Catholic Devotion
For Catholics, the **Assumption** is a source of great hope and comfort. It affirms the **Church's belief in the resurrection of the body** and provides an example of what awaits those who remain faithful to God. The **feast of the Assumption**, celebrated on **August 15**, is a day of joy and reverence, calling Catholics to reflect on the promise of eternal life and to honor Mary's pivotal role in salvation history.

---

3. The Relationship Between the Immaculate Conception and the Assumption

While the **Immaculate Conception** and the **Assumption** are distinct doctrines, they are deeply connected in Catholic theology. Both teachings highlight Mary's **unique relationship with God** and her role in salvation history. Together, they paint a picture of the fullness of **grace** and **holiness** that Mary embodies.

- **The Immaculate Conception** underscores Mary's **freedom from sin** and her special role as the **Mother of God**, while the **Assumption** celebrates her **eternal reward** as a result of that unique role and her life of holiness.

- The **Immaculate Conception** emphasizes that Mary was preserved from original sin to be a pure vessel for the Incarnation of Jesus Christ, and the **Assumption** confirms that this purity extends beyond her earthly life, to be taken **body and soul** into heaven.

Together, these doctrines reveal the **comprehensive holiness** of Mary—both her **sinlessness** in life and her **glorious transformation** into heaven. They also point to the ultimate **hope** of every Christian: that through God's grace, we too can be freed from sin and share in the fullness of eternal life in heaven.

---

4. The Impact of the Immaculate Conception and the Assumption on Catholic Spirituality

A Call to Holiness
Both the **Immaculate Conception** and the **Assumption** serve as profound reminders of the **possibility of holiness** for all believers. While these doctrines highlight Mary's **unique role**, they also serve to inspire Catholics to pursue a life of holiness through God's grace. Just as Mary was preserved from sin and taken into heaven, the faithful are called to cooperate with God's grace to live lives of **purity**, **obedience**, and **love**.

A Model of Trust in God's Plan
Mary's life exemplifies complete **trust** in God's plan. Her acceptance of God's will, even in the face of uncertainty and suffering, serves as a model for all Christians. Catholics believe that through the **Immaculate Conception**, God prepared Mary for this trust, and through the **Assumption**, He rewards her for her unwavering faith. These doctrines invite Catholics to trust in God's promises and to live their lives with the hope that one day, they too will experience the fullness of eternal life with God.

The doctrines of the **Immaculate Conception** and the **Assumption** celebrate Mary's **unique role** in salvation history and offer profound insights into the nature of **grace**, **holiness**, and **eternal life**. By preserving Mary from original sin and raising her into heaven, God underscores the **power of His grace** to transform human lives and assures the faithful of the ultimate victory over death. These teachings inspire Catholics to live lives of holiness, trusting in God's plan for them and hoping in the resurrection of the body. Through Mary's example and intercession, the faithful are drawn closer to the grace that makes all things possible.

Devotion to Mary and the Saints

In Catholicism, devotion to **Mary** and the **saints** holds a significant place, as these holy men and women serve as models of holiness, intercessors, and guides for the faithful. While the Catholic Church teaches that **worship** is reserved for **God alone**, the veneration of Mary and the saints is an important aspect of Catholic spiritual life. This devotion is not about **worshiping** them but honoring their lives and asking for their **intercession** before God.

This chapter explores the **role of devotion** to Mary and the saints in Catholic faith, how it is expressed, and the spiritual benefits it provides. Through understanding the nature of this devotion, Catholics are invited to deepen their **relationship with God**, growing in virtue, holiness, and trust in His grace.

---

1. The Nature of Devotion to Mary and the Saints

Honoring, Not Worshiping

Catholic devotion to **Mary** and the saints is an expression of **respect**, **love**, and **recognition** of their exemplary lives. The key distinction in Catholic teaching is that **worship** is reserved for God alone—Father, Son, and Holy Spirit. Mary and the saints are venerated, not worshiped, because they are **models of faith** who have lived lives of **holiness** and **obedience** to God.

The term **veneration** is used to describe the honor and reverence given to Mary and the saints. It is through their intercession that Catholics believe they are brought closer to God, as they ask the saints to pray for them and help them grow in virtue and holiness. The distinction between **veneration** (giving honor) and **adoration** (worship) ensures that Catholics recognize the **primary role of God** in salvation, while also honoring those who have faithfully followed His call.

The Communion of Saints

Catholics believe in the **communion of saints**, a theological concept that emphasizes the **spiritual bond** between all members of the Church—both living and deceased. This community is united in Christ and includes the saints in heaven, who continue to pray for and intercede on behalf of the living. In this communion, the faithful find **strength** and **comfort**, knowing that they are part of a **universal family** of believers who support one another in faith and prayer.

---

2. Devotion to Mary: The Mother of the Church

Mary's Special Role
In Catholicism, **Mary** holds a unique and honored position as the **Mother of God** and the **Mother of the Church**. Catholics believe that she was chosen by God to be the vessel through which the **Word became flesh** in the person of **Jesus Christ**. Mary's role in salvation history is unparalleled, and her **faith**, **humility**, and **obedience** make her the perfect model of what it means to follow Christ.

Catholic devotion to Mary is rooted in the belief that she is not only the **Mother of Jesus** but also a **spiritual mother** to all Christians. As the **Mother of the Church**, Mary is seen as one who lovingly cares for all the faithful, intercedes for them, and guides them closer to Christ. Catholics do not worship Mary, but rather honor her as the **first disciple**, who said **"yes"** to God and led others to follow His will.

Marian Devotions
Devotion to Mary is expressed in various **prayers**, **feast days**, and **spiritual practices** that help the faithful grow closer to her and to God. Some of the key expressions of Marian devotion include:

- **The Rosary**: One of the most well-known Catholic devotions, the Rosary is a prayer that focuses on the life of **Jesus Christ** through the intercession of Mary. It involves the repetition of prayers like the **Hail Mary**, the **Our Father**, and the **Glory Be**, while meditating on the key events in the lives of Christ and Mary called the **Mysteries**.

- **The Angelus**: A prayer that recalls the **Annunciation** (when the angel Gabriel announced to Mary that she would conceive the Son of God). It is often prayed three times a day, morning, noon, and evening.

- **Feast Days**: There are numerous feast days dedicated to Mary, such as the **Feast of the Immaculate Conception** (December 8), **The Assumption** (August 15), and **Our Lady of Guadalupe** (December 12). These days are celebrated with special liturgies, prayers, and processions.

- **The Magnificat**: This is a prayer of praise that Mary recited in **Luke 1:46-55**, where she gives glory to God for His greatness and His mercy towards her. This prayer is often recited in Catholic devotionals.

The Role of Mary in Intercession

Catholics believe that **Mary's intercession** is powerful because she is the **Mother of Jesus**. Just as a mother intercedes for her children, Mary intercedes for the faithful, asking her Son to show mercy and grace. Catholics turn to Mary in times of need, asking her to pray for them and to help them grow in their relationship with God. Through the **Hail Mary** and other Marian prayers, the faithful entrust their needs to Mary, trusting that her intercession will bring them closer to Christ.

---

3. Devotion to the Saints: Models of Faith and Intercessors

The Role of Saints

The **saints** are those men and women who have lived lives of extraordinary faith and virtue. They serve as **models** of holiness, demonstrating what it means to live a life completely dedicated to God. The saints come from all walks of life and include people from every age, race, and background. They provide unique examples of how to follow Christ in various circumstances, whether in the midst of persecution, poverty, or in the challenges of everyday life.

The Saints as Intercessors
Catholics believe that the saints, especially those who are in heaven, are powerful **intercessors**. Because they are now in God's presence, they are believed to be able to pray for the needs of the faithful with great efficacy. Catholics ask the saints to intercede on their behalf, just as one might ask a friend or family member to pray for them. The saints' unique relationship with God gives them the ability to help bring the petitions of the faithful before God.

There are specific saints associated with particular causes, such as:

- **Saint Jude**: The patron saint of hopeless causes.
- **Saint Therese of Lisieux**: Known for her "Little Way" of holiness, and many seek her intercession for matters of faith and hope.
- **Saint Anthony of Padua**: Patron of lost things, invoked for help finding lost items or finding direction in life.

The idea of **saints as intercessors** is not about worshiping the saints, but about seeking their **prayers** and **support** in one's own spiritual journey. Catholics believe that the saints, because of their holiness, have a unique ability to present the prayers of the faithful to God.

---

4. The Role of Relics and Pilgrimages in Marian and Saintly Devotion

Relics
A **relic** is a physical object or part of a saint's body that is venerated by the faithful. The Church teaches that these relics are sacred because they are connected to the holiness of the saint and their unique relationship with God. Catholics may visit shrines or churches that house the relics of saints as an expression of devotion and a way of connecting more deeply to their lives of faith.

Relics can be categorized into:

- **First-class relics**: Parts of the saint's body, such as bones or blood.
- **Second-class relics**: Items used by the saint, such as their clothing or possessions.
- **Third-class relics**: Items that have been touched to a first-class relic.

Catholics believe that relics serve as **tangible signs** of the holiness of the saints, and that veneration of relics can bring blessings, healing, and grace.

Pilgrimages
Pilgrimages to sites associated with Mary or the saints are a traditional form of devotion. **Lourdes**, **Fatima**, and **Rome** are some of the most famous pilgrimage destinations where Catholics can visit relics, shrines, and other holy sites. Pilgrimages are a way of honoring the saints and seeking **spiritual renewal**, **penance**, and the **grace** of God. It is an act of faith, where the journey itself can be seen as a symbol of the Christian pilgrimage toward eternal life.

---

5. The Spiritual Benefits of Devotion to Mary and the Saints

Growth in Holiness
Devotion to Mary and the saints is a way for Catholics to grow in holiness. By imitating their lives and virtues, Catholics are encouraged to **grow in virtue**, **trust in God**, and **serve others** with love and humility. The saints provide examples of how to live out the **Gospel** in practical, everyday ways, and their prayers help the faithful remain focused on the **path of righteousness**.

Increased Faith and Hope
Mary and the saints, as models of faith, remind Catholics that it is possible to live a life of **complete surrender** to God's will. Their

intercession also brings hope, as Catholics trust in the saints' prayers and in God's ultimate plan of salvation. The saints show that **perseverance in faith** through trials leads to the promise of eternal life.

Devotion to **Mary** and the **saints** is an essential part of Catholic spiritual life. By venerating these holy figures and asking for their intercession, Catholics are encouraged to live out the virtues they exemplified and to grow closer to God. Mary and the saints are not worshiped but honored as examples of how to follow Christ and as intercessors who bring the petitions of the faithful before God. Through their devotion, Catholics are strengthened in their faith and inspired to live lives of holiness, service, and love.

Chapter 9: Moral Teachings and Catholic Ethics

The Ten Commandments: A Path to Righteous Living

The **Ten Commandments**, also known as the **Decalogue**, are a set of **ethical guidelines** given by God to the Israelites on Mount Sinai, as recorded in the **Book of Exodus** and reiterated in the **Book of Deuteronomy**. These commandments are not only central to Jewish and Christian faiths but also serve as timeless principles for living a righteous and just life. In Catholicism, the Ten Commandments are viewed as the foundation of **moral law**, providing clear guidance on how to love and honor God and others.

In this chapter, we will explore each of the **Ten Commandments**, their **biblical significance**, and how they serve as a moral compass for the faithful. By understanding the Commandments as more than mere rules, Catholics are invited to embrace them as a **path to holiness** and **righteous living** that leads to true peace and harmony with God and others.

---

1. The First Commandment: "I am the Lord your God: you shall not have strange gods before me."

Faithfulness to God
The **First Commandment** calls us to worship God alone, rejecting all idols and false gods. In a world filled with distractions and competing desires, this commandment reminds believers to place God at the center of their lives and to prioritize their relationship with Him. Catholics interpret this commandment as an invitation to trust in God's **sovereignty**, to rely on His grace, and to reject anything that might take His place in our hearts.

This commandment calls us to reflect on our own **idols**, which can include materialism, fame, power, or even relationships, and to purify our hearts to worship God alone. **Faithfulness to God** is the foundation of a righteous life because it establishes the relationship that all other commandments build upon.

Living the First Commandment

- **Loving God** with all your heart, soul, and mind.
- **Rejecting idolatry**, which includes placing excessive value on wealth, power, or self-centered ambitions.
- **Prayer** and regular worship are vital for nurturing a relationship with God and making Him the center of life.

---

2. The Second Commandment: "You shall not take the name of the Lord your God in vain."

Respect for God's Name

The **Second Commandment** teaches respect for God's holy name. Taking God's name in vain means using it irreverently, carelessly, or in a manner that dishonors His sacredness. This commandment calls believers to a life of reverence, not only for God Himself but also for the **sacred things** related to God, such as the **Scriptures**, the **sacraments**, and the **church**.

Catholics are taught that speaking the name of God should be done with **respect**, **awe**, and **reverence**. This includes avoiding **blasphemy**, **cursing**, or using God's name in **vain oaths** or trivial expressions.

Living the Second Commandment

- **Honor God's name** in prayer, speech, and in daily life.
- **Speak with reverence** about God, avoiding irreverence and blasphemy.

- **Use God's name** to bless, praise, and pray rather than misuse it in a casual or disrespectful way.

---

3. The Third Commandment: "Remember the sabbath day, to keep it holy."

Rest and Worship

The **Third Commandment** calls for a day of rest and worship, recognizing the **Sabbath** as a sacred time. For Catholics, this is primarily observed on **Sunday**, the day of the **Resurrection of Christ**. Observing the Sabbath is not just about abstaining from work but about dedicating time to **God** through **worship**, **prayer**, **family**, and **rest**.

This commandment highlights the need for a regular spiritual rhythm in life—taking time away from daily distractions to **renew the body**, **refresh the soul**, and deepen one's relationship with God. The celebration of the **Mass** on Sundays is an integral part of fulfilling this commandment.

Living the Third Commandment

- **Attend Mass** regularly, especially on Sundays, to honor God.
- **Rest from unnecessary labor** on Sundays, allowing time for prayer and reflection.
- Use Sundays to engage in **spiritual activities** such as prayer, reflection, and acts of charity.

---

4. The Fourth Commandment: "Honor your father and your mother."

Respect for Authority and Family

The **Fourth Commandment** emphasizes the importance of respecting **parents** and those in authority. Honoring one's father and mother is not merely about obedience but also about showing **gratitude**, **love**, and **respect** for the sacrifices and guidance they provide. This commandment establishes the foundation for respecting **authority** in all aspects of life—family, government, and the Church.

Catholics believe that the family is a **domestic Church**, where children are taught how to love and serve God. Therefore, honoring parents is integral to living a life of faith, as it is the first school where faith and values are learned.

Living the Fourth Commandment

- **Respect** and **care for your parents** and family members.
- **Obey legitimate authority** in the family, society, and the Church.
- Support and encourage the **well-being** of parents, especially in their old age.

---

5. The Fifth Commandment: "You shall not kill."

Respect for Life

The **Fifth Commandment** is a call to respect and protect the **sanctity of life**. It forbids murder, but its meaning extends beyond just the act of killing to include anything that causes harm to others, such as **anger**, **hatred**, and **violence**. Catholics believe that every human life is a **gift from God** and should be treated with the utmost dignity and respect from conception to natural death.

This commandment also challenges believers to work toward a **culture of life** that respects not only physical life but also emotional and spiritual well-being, promoting peace, reconciliation, and forgiveness.

Living the Fifth Commandment

- Avoid **violence** and **anger**, promoting peace and **non-violence**.
- **Respect the dignity of all life**, including the elderly, unborn, and vulnerable.
- Advocate for the **protection of life** through prayer, charity, and justice.

---

6. The Sixth Commandment: "You shall not commit adultery."

Chastity and Fidelity

The **Sixth Commandment** speaks to the importance of **fidelity** in marriage and **chastity** in all relationships. It underscores the sacredness of the marital relationship and calls for purity and integrity in **sexual relations**. For Catholics, this commandment highlights the need for **respect for the dignity** of each person and for the **sanctity of marriage** as a sacrament.

This commandment also challenges believers to lead lives of **self-control** and **respect**, avoiding lust, infidelity, and the objectification of others. It calls for a respect for the **whole person** rather than reducing people to objects for selfish gratification.

Living the Sixth Commandment

- **Be faithful** in marriage and relationships, honoring the commitment made to one's spouse.
- **Practice chastity** in thought, word, and deed.
- **Guard your heart and mind** against temptation and impurity.

---

7. The Seventh Commandment: "You shall not steal."

Honesty and Justice
The **Seventh Commandment** forbids stealing, but it also calls for a life of **honesty**, **integrity**, and **justice** in all dealings. It teaches that material possessions and wealth are gifts from God and should not be taken unjustly. Catholics believe in the **right to private property** but also in the duty to **share** and use one's resources for the **common good**, especially to assist the poor and needy.

This commandment encourages Catholics to live lives of **generosity** and **fairness**, always acting with justice and avoiding greed and exploitation.

Living the Seventh Commandment

- **Respect others' property** and avoid cheating, theft, or fraud.
- Be **generous** with what you have, supporting those in need.
- **Act justly** in all financial and material transactions.

---

8. The Eighth Commandment: "You shall not bear false witness against your neighbor."

Truthfulness and Integrity
The **Eighth Commandment** calls for **truthfulness** in speech and action. It forbids lying, gossiping, slander, and misrepresentation of others, especially in matters of **justice** and **testimony**. Catholics believe that speaking the truth is essential to living in harmony with others and building trust within the community.

This commandment calls believers to be **honest**, to avoid misleading others, and to **safeguard the reputation** of others, always speaking in ways that build up and encourage.

Living the Eighth Commandment

- **Speak the truth** in all situations, avoiding lies and deceit.
- **Guard the reputation** of others by avoiding gossip and slander.
- Be a source of **encouragement** and **support** for others.

---

9. The Ninth Commandment: "You shall not covet your neighbor's wife."

Purity of Heart and Mind

The **Ninth Commandment** addresses the issue of **desire** and warns against **coveting** what belongs to others, particularly in matters of **sexual purity**. It calls for **purity of heart**, urging the faithful to guard their thoughts and desires, and to avoid objectifying others.

Catholics are called to be **content** with what they have and to avoid seeking fulfillment in things that are contrary to **God's plan for love and marriage**.

Living the Ninth Commandment

- **Cultivate purity of heart** and mind by avoiding inappropriate desires.
- **Guard your thoughts** and **desires** and practice self-control.
- **Respect the dignity** of others, particularly in relationships.

---

10. The Tenth Commandment: "You shall not covet your neighbor's goods."

Contentment and Generosity

The **Tenth Commandment** warns against **coveting** the possessions of others. It teaches that true happiness does not come from accumulating wealth or material goods but from a **grateful heart** and a **generous spirit**. This commandment calls for **contentment** and **trust in God's provision**, rather than living a life driven by greed or envy.

It encourages the faithful to be **generous** with their resources, to support others, and to avoid excessive attachment to material possessions.

Living the Tenth Commandment

- **Practice contentment** with what you have and avoid envy.
- **Be generous** with your possessions, sharing with those in need.
- **Trust in God** to provide for your needs, avoiding excessive desire for material wealth.

The **Ten Commandments** offer a comprehensive path to righteous living by guiding believers in their relationship with God and others. They are not mere rules but invitations to **live in harmony**, **justice**, **truth**, and **love**. By embracing these commandments, Catholics can grow in **holiness**, align their lives with God's will, and become instruments of peace and justice in the world. Living according to the Ten Commandments leads to a life marked by **integrity**, **humility**, and **compassion**, ultimately drawing the faithful closer to God's divine plan for their lives.

The Catechism's Moral Guide

The **Catechism of the Catholic Church** serves as the foundational reference for understanding the teachings of the Catholic faith, encompassing beliefs, sacraments, prayer, and morals. Specifically, the section on **moral theology** offers a comprehensive guide to living a life that is aligned with God's will. The Catechism addresses how Catholics should act in various aspects of their lives, emphasizing both the **virtues** that should be cultivated and the **sins** that should be avoided in the pursuit of holiness.

This chapter explores the Catechism's teachings on **moral guidance**, providing insights into the Church's view on what it means to live a **righteous life**. From foundational concepts like the **dignity of the human person** to specific moral laws and teachings on **social justice**, the Catechism offers a practical guide to living out the Christian faith in daily life.

---

1. The Foundations of Catholic Moral Teaching

The Moral Law and Divine Law
At the heart of Catholic moral theology is the belief that **God is the ultimate source** of all moral law. **Divine Law**, which includes the **natural law** (understood through human reason) and **revealed law** (expressed through Scripture and the teachings of the Church), directs humans in how they should live according to God's will. Catholics believe that God's law is not arbitrary but is an expression of His **goodness** and **love** for humanity. By following God's laws, Catholics are invited into a deeper **relationship with Him**.

The **moral law** is an objective standard of right and wrong that is grounded in **human dignity** and the **common good**. It reveals what is truly good for people and helps them achieve their **ultimate end**, which is union with God in eternal life. The Catechism teaches that moral law is not just a set of rules, but a way to reflect God's love and the **call to holiness** that each person has received.

---

2. The Role of Conscience in Moral Decision-Making

What is Conscience?
Conscience is the **inner voice** within each person that helps guide decisions in line with what is good and just. The Catechism defines conscience as "a judgment of reason" whereby the human person recognizes the moral quality of an action, whether it be **right** or **wrong** (CCC 1778). It is a gift from God that enables people to discern God's will in concrete situations.

The Catechism emphasizes that conscience is not something that can be blindly followed but must be **formed and educated** in light of **truth** and **faith**. A well-formed conscience is aligned with the **natural law**, **Sacred Scripture**, and the **teachings of the Church**. This involves **personal reflection**, **prayer**, and a **desire to live morally** according to God's guidance.

The Formation of Conscience
Catholics are encouraged to form their consciences through:

- **Prayer**: Seeking God's guidance in decision-making.
- **Study of Scripture**: Understanding how God's Word applies to moral choices.
- **Church Teachings**: Relying on the wisdom of the Church and its moral guidelines.
- **Theological Virtues**: Cultivating **faith**, **hope**, and **charity** in one's daily actions.

An educated and well-formed conscience leads to the ability to make decisions that reflect God's goodness and will.

---

3. The Theological Virtues: The Foundation for Moral Living

The Catechism highlights the **theological virtues—faith**, **hope**, and **charity**—as the foundation for moral life. These virtues direct the believer's mind and heart toward God and His plan of salvation.

Faith
Faith is the virtue by which a person **believes** in God and His Word. It enables individuals to trust in God's promises and accept the truths revealed by Him, especially those revealed through **Christ and His Church**. The virtue of faith is the foundation of all other virtues, for it connects the believer directly to God and His divine wisdom.

Hope
Hope is the virtue that **directs the heart toward the eternal life promised by God**. It enables the believer to remain steadfast in faith, trusting that God's promises are true, even amidst suffering and difficulty. Hope is not passive but involves an active desire to cooperate with God's grace in the journey toward eternal life.

Charity (Love)
Charity is the greatest of the theological virtues, as it involves loving God above all things and loving one's neighbor as oneself. Charity compels individuals to act selflessly, with **compassion** and **service** toward others. It is the virtue that reflects God's nature most clearly, for God is love (1 John 4:8), and it is through charity that Christians are called to manifest His love in the world.

---

4. The Cardinal Virtues: Practical Guidance for Everyday Life

The **cardinal virtues—prudence**, **justice**, **fortitude**, and **temperance**—are moral virtues that help individuals navigate the complexities of daily life and make decisions that reflect their Christian faith.

Prudence

Prudence is the virtue that allows individuals to make sound **judgments** and decisions. It is not simply a matter of choosing wisely, but of seeking **God's will** in every situation. Prudence involves **discernment**, carefully weighing the options before making a decision, and acting with foresight and caution.

Justice

Justice is the virtue that directs a person to **give others their due**, whether that is respect, fairness, or a proper share of resources. Justice in the moral sense goes beyond legal justice to encompass the **duty to care for others**, especially the most vulnerable in society.

Fortitude

Fortitude is the virtue that allows individuals to **persevere in the face of challenges** and remain steadfast in their faith. This virtue is essential for enduring **suffering**, resisting **temptation**, and staying true to God's commandments, even when it is difficult.

Temperance

Temperance is the virtue that helps individuals **moderate their desires** and actions, avoiding excess. It teaches Catholics to exercise **self-control** over the passions, whether that be in regard to **food**, **drink**, or **material possessions**. Temperance is essential for maintaining balance in life and avoiding the snares of **greed** or **overindulgence**.

---

5. The Ten Commandments: A Guide to Moral Living

The **Ten Commandments** serve as the moral foundation for living a life of **obedience** to God and **respect** for others. The Catechism teaches that the Ten Commandments are not just historical laws but timeless moral principles that reflect the **natural law** written on the human heart. By following the commandments, Catholics are called to live in harmony with God's will.

1. **Love God above all things.**

2. **Honor God's name.**
3. **Keep holy the Sabbath.**
4. **Honor your father and mother.**
5. **Do not kill.**
6. **Do not commit adultery.**
7. **Do not steal.**
8. **Do not bear false witness against your neighbor.**
9. **Do not covet your neighbor's wife.**
10. **Do not covet your neighbor's goods.**

The Catechism teaches that living by these commandments leads to **righteous living** and helps build a **just society**. They are not just prohibitions but invitations to live in the **freedom** that comes from following God's plan.

---

6. Sin and Reconciliation: The Path to Moral Healing

The Catechism addresses the reality of **sin** in human life and its destructive effects on the moral order. **Sin** is seen as a failure to live according to the moral law and to act in **harmony** with God's will.

Types of Sin

- **Mortal Sin**: A grave violation of God's law that destroys the life of grace within a person and separates them from God.

- **Venial Sin**: Less serious offenses that damage the relationship with God but do not sever it completely.

The Catechism emphasizes the importance of **reconciliation** through the **sacrament of confession** for healing from sin and restoring one's moral integrity. Through **repentance** and **confession**, individuals are forgiven and restored to grace, enabling them to continue their journey toward holiness.

---

7. The Social Doctrine of the Church: Living Out Moral Teaching in Society

The Church's moral teachings are not confined to personal behavior but extend to **social justice** and the **common good**. The Catechism presents a **moral framework** for addressing issues like **poverty**, **immigration**, **healthcare**, and **human rights**, urging Catholics to work for a society that reflects **human dignity** and the **justice** of God.

Catholic moral teaching encourages the faithful to engage in actions that promote the **well-being** of all people, especially the poor and marginalized, and to challenge systems of **injustice** or **exploitation**.

The **Catechism's moral guide** provides a clear and comprehensive framework for living a life of virtue, integrity, and holiness. Rooted in **divine law** and the teachings of **Jesus Christ**, it invites Catholics to grow in their relationship with God by making decisions that reflect His goodness and love. By following the moral teachings of the Church, individuals are called to live lives of **righteousness**, **justice**, and **compassion**, making a real difference in their own lives and in the world around them. The Catechism's moral guidance helps the faithful understand how to live in accordance with God's will, leading to the fulfillment of their **ultimate purpose**—union with God in eternal life.

Conscience, Sin, and Reconciliation

In Catholicism, the concepts of **conscience**, **sin**, and **reconciliation** are central to the believer's journey toward holiness and spiritual growth. These elements shape the moral life by offering guidance on how to live in accordance with God's will, how to respond when we fall short, and how to restore our relationship with God and others. Understanding these concepts is essential for any Catholic seeking to live a life of **virtue** and **faithfulness**.

This chapter explores the profound connection between conscience, sin, and reconciliation, drawing from the teachings of the **Catechism of the Catholic Church** to illuminate their meaning, importance, and practical application in daily life. By recognizing the role of conscience in moral decision-making, acknowledging the reality of sin, and embracing the sacrament of reconciliation, Catholics are empowered to grow in holiness and remain in union with God.

---

1. Conscience: The Voice of God in Our Hearts

The Nature of Conscience

Conscience is described in the **Catechism** as the "inner voice" that helps individuals discern the moral quality of their actions. It is a judgment of reason that helps one recognize the good and avoid the evil in particular situations (CCC 1778). Catholics believe that **conscience** is a gift from God, which allows human beings to know the **moral law** written in their hearts. This awareness is in harmony with **natural law**, which is accessible to human reason, and **divine law**, which is revealed through Scripture and Church teachings.

Conscience is not merely a **feeling** or a **subjective instinct**; rather, it is a rational, moral compass that is rooted in objective truth. It plays a crucial role in helping individuals choose the **good** and avoid the **evil**. The **Catechism** emphasizes that **conscience** requires constant formation through prayer, reflection, and study of Scripture and Church teachings.

Forming a Good Conscience

The Catholic Church teaches that a person's conscience must be formed properly to make sound moral decisions. This formation requires:

- **Prayer**: Seeking God's guidance and strength.
- **Study of Scripture**: Understanding God's Word as it applies to daily life.
- **Study of Church Teachings**: Learning the Church's moral and doctrinal principles.
- **Theological Virtues**: Cultivating **faith**, **hope**, and **charity**, which empower the individual to act in accordance with God's will.

A well-formed conscience helps the individual recognize when they have failed to live up to God's standards and invites them to turn to God in repentance and reconciliation.

---

2. Sin: The Breakdown of Relationship with God

What is Sin?

In Catholic theology, **sin** is any act, word, or thought that goes against **God's law** and separates us from His love. The **Catechism** defines sin as "an offense against reason, truth, and right conscience" (CCC 1849). Sin involves choosing something that is **not aligned** with God's will and breaking the relationship with Him. It can be **mortal** or **venial**, depending on the seriousness of the offense and the effect it has on one's relationship with God.

- **Mortal Sin**: A grave offense that destroys the **life of grace** in the soul, completely severing the relationship with God. Mortal sins involve three key elements: **grave matter**, **full knowledge**, and **deliberate consent**. Examples include murder, adultery, and blasphemy.

- **Venial Sin**: A less serious offense that weakens the relationship with God but does not sever it completely. Venial sins involve less serious matters or lack one of the three elements of mortal sin. While venial sins do not result in the loss of **sanctifying grace**, they can make a person more susceptible to committing mortal sin.

The Effects of Sin

Sin has profound consequences, not only on the individual but also on the **community**. It disrupts personal peace, spiritual harmony, and social justice. Sin also has a ripple effect on relationships with others, leading to **broken trust**, **harm**, and **division**. Most importantly, sin alienates the person from God, who is the source of all life and grace.

However, **the Catechism** emphasizes that God's **love and mercy** are greater than any sin, and He invites the sinner to seek **forgiveness** and **reconciliation**.

---

3. The Sacrament of Reconciliation: Restoring the Broken Relationship

The Need for Reconciliation

The Church teaches that the **sacrament of reconciliation**, also known as **confession**, is the means by which a person can be reconciled with God after sinning. Through this sacrament, Catholics receive the forgiveness of their sins and the grace needed to grow in holiness. The sacrament is a gift of **God's mercy**, which restores the individual to a state of grace and heals the damage caused by sin.

The Catechism teaches that **reconciliation** is essential for **spiritual healing**. Through it, one acknowledges their sin, expresses sorrow, and receives absolution from a priest, who acts as a representative of Christ and the Church. The priest's role is not to judge but to serve as an instrument of God's forgiveness.

The Three Key Elements of Reconciliation

1. **Contrition**: The first step toward reconciliation is genuine **sorrow** for one's sins. Contrition involves a sincere desire to be restored to God and a commitment to avoid sin in the future. There are two types of contrition:

    - **Perfect Contrition**: Sorrow for sin based on love for God and the desire to be reconciled with Him.

    - **Imperfect Contrition**: Sorrow for sin due to fear of punishment or the consequences of sin, but still a step toward healing.

2. **Confession**: The second step is **confessing sins** to a priest in the sacrament of reconciliation. The individual must confess all **mortal sins** and any serious matters to ensure they are properly absolved. The priest listens and offers counsel, helping the penitent to understand the gravity of sin and the grace available through God.

3. **Penance**: The final step involves performing the **penance** given by the priest, which may include prayers, acts of charity, or sacrifices. This helps the individual to make amends for their sins and express gratitude for the grace received through the sacrament.

The Grace of the Sacrament

The sacrament of reconciliation restores the **life of grace** in the soul, healing the wounds caused by sin. It strengthens the individual to resist future temptation and deepens the relationship with God. Through this sacrament, the Church offers a tangible encounter with God's mercy and compassion, reminding the faithful that no sin is too great to be forgiven.

---

4. The Role of Conscience in Reconciliation

A well-formed conscience plays a crucial role in the process of reconciliation. Conscience helps the individual **recognize** their sin, prompting them to seek God's forgiveness. The **Catechism** teaches that a person must examine their conscience regularly to identify areas of their life that need healing. Conscience guides the person to make a **moral inventory** of their actions, thoughts, and attitudes, allowing them to approach the sacrament of reconciliation with sincerity and a deep desire for renewal.

In the process of reconciliation, Catholics are encouraged to make a **personal examination of conscience** before confession, reflecting on their actions in light of the **Ten Commandments**, the **Beatitudes**, and the teachings of the Church. This allows the penitent to approach God with humility and repentance, seeking true conversion and the strength to live a more faithful life.

---

5. The Power of Reconciliation: Healing and Restoration

Reconciliation is not only about **forgiveness** but also about **restoration**. Through the sacrament, individuals experience a profound sense of **peace** and **spiritual healing**. The **Catechism** teaches that the peace that comes from the sacrament is a reflection of God's love and mercy. It is a reminder that God is always ready to welcome back His children who have strayed.

Furthermore, reconciliation helps the believer to grow in **spiritual maturity** by providing an opportunity for **conversion**—a continual process of turning toward God and away from sin. The grace received through confession enables the individual to **live a more virtuous life**, free from the chains of sin and fully aligned with God's will.

Living in Reconciliation

Living in reconciliation means continuing to walk in **God's grace** and actively seeking to live a life of **holiness**. It means being vigilant about one's conscience, seeking forgiveness when needed, and striving to grow in love and virtue. Reconciliation with God is not a one-time event but an ongoing invitation to deepen the relationship with God and to live in communion with others.

Conscience, sin, and reconciliation are central to the Catholic understanding of moral living. Conscience is the inner guide that directs the individual toward moral choices, while sin represents the breakdown in the relationship with God and others. The sacrament of reconciliation offers the path to healing, forgiveness, and spiritual restoration. By embracing the grace of reconciliation, Catholics are called to live lives of repentance, humility, and continuous conversion, growing in holiness and drawing ever closer to the love of God.

Chapter 10: Growing in Faith and Becoming a Fully Participating Catholic

The Rite of Christian Initiation for Adults (RCIA)

The **Rite of Christian Initiation for Adults (RCIA)** is the process through which adults are initiated into the **Catholic Church**. It is a journey of **conversion**, **growth**, and **faith development**, guiding individuals through the essential teachings, traditions, and practices of the Catholic faith. The RCIA is a spiritual formation process that culminates in the reception of the **Sacraments of Initiation**: **Baptism**, **Eucharist**, and **Confirmation**.

For those seeking to enter the Church, RCIA offers a structured way to deepen their understanding of the faith, build a relationship with God, and become full members of the Church. It is also an opportunity for **renewal** for those who may already be baptized in another Christian tradition but seek full communion with the Catholic Church.

This chapter explores the RCIA process, its structure, key rituals, and its significance in the life of the Church, helping potential converts and those accompanying them understand the spiritual and doctrinal importance of this rite.

---

1. Overview of RCIA: A Journey of Faith

The RCIA is designed for adults who are not yet baptized, those who have been baptized in another Christian tradition but wish to join the Catholic Church, and those who have not yet received the Sacrament of Confirmation. It is an **invitation to faith** and a deepening of one's relationship with **Jesus Christ** and His Church.

The process of RCIA is **gradual**, allowing individuals to explore the meaning of faith, grow in spiritual understanding, and make an informed decision about joining the Church. It is a journey of both **teaching** and **prayer**, providing an opportunity for candidates to reflect on their personal relationship with God and their place within the Christian community.

2. Stages of the RCIA Process

The RCIA is typically divided into several stages, each marked by distinct liturgical rites and spiritual milestones. These stages are designed to guide the participant through different aspects of their faith journey, preparing them for the full reception of the sacraments.

1. Period of Inquiry (Pre-Catechumenate)

The **Period of Inquiry** is the initial stage of the RCIA process. It is a time of exploration and questioning, where individuals who are curious about the Catholic faith are invited to ask questions and learn more about what it means to be a follower of Christ.

- **Focus**: This period is centered around **personal discernment**—individuals reflect on their desire to know God more deeply and consider whether they feel called to join the Catholic Church.
- **Participants**: Those who are curious about the Catholic faith or have a desire to become Catholic but are unsure.
- **Goal**: To provide basic information about the Catholic faith, answer questions, and allow participants to reflect on their spiritual journey. At the end of this period, candidates decide whether to continue their journey toward baptism and full initiation.

2. The Catechumenate

Once an individual decides to pursue membership in the Church, they enter the **Catechumenate**. This stage is more focused on **spiritual formation** and catechesis (religious instruction). Catechumens (those preparing for baptism) are formally welcomed into the Church community and are introduced to the **teachings** and **sacraments** of the Catholic faith.

- **Focus**: The Catechumenate is a period of **intense formation** in the teachings of the Church. It includes regular **Bible study**, **prayer**, and **discussion** of the Church's core beliefs and practices.

- **Participants**: Those who have decided to become baptized members of the Church (catechumens) and those who are already baptized but seeking to complete their initiation with Confirmation and Eucharist.

- **Goal**: To prepare individuals to receive the Sacraments of Initiation through reflection on the Word of God and learning about the nature of Christian life.

3. The Period of Purification and Enlightenment

The **Period of Purification and Enlightenment** is the final stage of preparation before the reception of the Sacraments of Initiation. This period usually coincides with **Lent**, the season of repentance and spiritual renewal in the Church. It is a time of reflection, **introspection**, and **prayer** to purify the candidates' hearts and minds in preparation for the Easter Vigil, when they will receive the sacraments.

- **Focus**: This stage is characterized by **spiritual preparation** and **penance**, with a deepening commitment to prayer and fasting. Candidates are encouraged to examine their lives and seek reconciliation with God and others.

- **Rites**: The key rites during this period are the **Scrutinies**, which are prayers of **intercession** and **blessing** meant to help the candidates face any lingering obstacles to receiving the sacraments. These rites are celebrated on the **third, fourth**, and **fifth Sundays of Lent**.

- **Goal**: To help candidates experience a deeper sense of **spiritual renewal**, purification, and readiness to fully receive the Sacraments of Initiation.

4. The Sacraments of Initiation

The culmination of the RCIA process occurs at the **Easter Vigil**, where candidates receive the Sacraments of Initiation: **Baptism**, **Confirmation**, and **Eucharist**.

- **Baptism**: For those who are not yet baptized, baptism is the sacrament that marks their entry into the Catholic Church. It involves the pouring of water over the candidate's head (or immersion) and the invocation of the Holy Trinity.
- **Confirmation**: The candidates are then **confirmed** by the bishop or priest, receiving the gifts of the Holy Spirit to strengthen their faith and empower them to live a Christian life.
- **Eucharist**: Finally, the candidates receive the **Eucharist** for the first time, participating fully in the Body and Blood of Christ.

---

3. The Rite of Christian Initiation: Key Rituals and Rites

Throughout the RCIA process, participants experience a series of key rituals that help mark important spiritual milestones and transitions. These rituals provide a deep connection to the Church's tradition and help to immerse participants in the liturgical life of the Church.

The Rite of Acceptance

This rite marks the first official step for catechumens into the Church community. It is usually celebrated on a Sunday during Mass and includes a public acknowledgment of the candidates' desire to seek baptism and membership in the Church. The rite includes prayers of blessing and the signing of the catechumens' foreheads, symbolizing their commitment to Christ.

The Rite of Election

The Rite of Election is celebrated on the First Sunday of Lent. It is a significant event where the bishop officially "elects" the catechumens for baptism. This rite marks the transition from the catechumenate stage to the period of purification and enlightenment.

The Scrutinies

These are rites of **purification** and **enlightenment** that are celebrated on the third, fourth, and fifth Sundays of Lent. They consist of prayers and exorcisms, helping the catechumens confront and overcome any obstacles to their journey toward baptism.

---

4. Post-Initiation: Mystagogy

After the reception of the Sacraments of Initiation, the new Catholics enter a period called **Mystagogy**. This period is dedicated to deepening their understanding of the sacraments they have received, particularly the **Eucharist**, and growing more fully into their role as members of the Church. Mystagogy takes place during the **Easter season**, the time following their initiation, and is an opportunity for reflection, spiritual growth, and integration into the Church community.

- **Focus**: Reflection on the sacramental life, particularly on the meaning of the **Eucharist** and the **mission** of being a disciple of Christ.
- **Goal**: To deepen the spiritual life of the neophytes (new members) and help them find their place in the community as full members of the Church.

---

5. The Importance of RCIA in the Church

RCIA plays a pivotal role in the life of the Catholic Church. It is not merely a set of rituals but an **invitation to a lifelong journey of faith**.

The process fosters spiritual growth, community integration, and an understanding of the profound love of God as expressed through the Catholic Church. It also emphasizes the communal nature of the Church, encouraging candidates to participate in the **liturgy**, **sacraments**, and the **life of service**.

For the entire Church, the RCIA process is a reminder of the **call to evangelize** and invite others to experience the life-changing grace of God. As new members are welcomed into the Church, the community itself is renewed and strengthened, reaffirming its mission to proclaim the **Gospel** to the world.

The **Rite of Christian Initiation for Adults (RCIA)** is a profound and transformative journey for those seeking to enter the Catholic Church. It is a process of learning, conversion, and growth in faith, culminating in the reception of the sacraments of baptism, confirmation, and the Eucharist. Through this process, individuals are invited to experience the fullness of the Christian life, building a relationship with Christ and the Church. RCIA is a reminder of the Church's role in welcoming all to the community of faith and walking alongside them as they respond to God's call to be His disciples.

Becoming Involved in the Catholic Community

One of the most powerful aspects of Catholicism is the strong sense of **community** and **belonging** that exists within the Church. Being Catholic is not just about individual belief or personal piety; it's about being part of a global family of faith that is deeply connected through worship, service, and shared commitment to Christ. Becoming involved in the **Catholic community** allows a person to grow in their faith, develop relationships with others who share similar values, and contribute to the mission of the Church.

This chapter will explore various ways to become more deeply involved in the Catholic community, both within the local parish and the broader Church. It will emphasize the importance of **participation** in the **sacramental life**, **service to others**, and **spiritual formation** as means of becoming an active and engaged member of the Catholic Church.

---

1. The Importance of Community in Catholic Life

The Catholic faith teaches that **community** is at the heart of the Church's mission. The Church is not just a collection of individuals but a living **body of Christ**, united in worship, service, and love. **Pope Francis** has often emphasized the importance of community, calling the Church a "community of communities" (Evangelii Gaudium, 28).

Being involved in the Catholic community is not just about fulfilling a duty, but about **responding to God's call** to live out the Gospel in the context of **relationships** and **shared responsibility**. Jesus Himself established the Church as a community, and He called His disciples to live together in love and service (John 13:34-35). The community is where we grow in **holiness**, deepen our **faith**, and live out our **vocation** as baptized Christians.

---

2. Participating in the Sacramental Life

The **sacraments** are the heart of Catholic life and provide an essential connection between individuals and the Church community. The most direct way to be involved in the Catholic community is by **participating regularly in the sacraments**, especially the **Eucharist**.

Eucharist: The Source and Summit of Catholic Life

The **Eucharist**, often referred to as **Holy Communion**, is the central act of Catholic worship. Catholics believe that in the Eucharist, they receive the **Body and Blood of Christ**, which strengthens them in their faith and unites them with the global Church. By attending **Mass regularly**, one not only participates in the liturgical life of the Church but also becomes part of the global family of faith that celebrates Christ's presence.

- **Daily or Weekly Mass Attendance**: Attending Mass is an essential way to grow spiritually and stay connected to the broader Catholic community. It is an opportunity to **praise God**, receive the **Eucharist**, and be nourished by the **Word of God**.

Confession: Healing and Renewal

The sacrament of **Reconciliation (Confession)** offers a way to be healed and restored to full communion with the Church. Regularly going to confession helps maintain a healthy spiritual life, removing obstacles to one's relationship with God and others. The community is strengthened when its members seek reconciliation with God and one another.

- **Participating in Confession**: Regular confession is essential for maintaining spiritual health and peace. It allows individuals to become more involved in the life of the Church, as the whole community is united in the call to repentance and forgiveness.

Other Sacraments

- **Baptism**: For those who have not yet been baptized, entering the community through the sacrament of baptism is the first step in becoming fully integrated into the Church.
- **Confirmation**: Confirming one's faith and commitment to the Church through the sacrament of Confirmation allows individuals to receive the **Holy Spirit** and become fully initiated members of the Catholic community.
- **Matrimony**: For couples, the sacrament of marriage strengthens their bond, making them an active part of the Church's mission through their shared vocation of love and service.
- **Holy Orders**: For those discerning a vocation to the priesthood or diaconate, Holy Orders is the sacrament that calls them to serve the community in a special way.

By regularly engaging in these sacraments, individuals strengthen their bond with the Church community and grow deeper in their faith.

---

3. Volunteering and Service to Others

One of the most meaningful ways to become involved in the Catholic community is by engaging in **service**. Catholicism places a strong emphasis on **serving others**, especially the **poor**, **vulnerable**, and **marginalized**. This commitment to service is rooted in the **teachings of Jesus**, who called His followers to feed the hungry, clothe the naked, and visit the sick (Matthew 25:35-40). Service is not just a duty; it is a **vocation** that reflects God's love for humanity.

Ways to Serve in the Catholic Community

- **Parish Ministries**: Every parish has numerous ways for individuals to get involved, such as serving as lectors, ushers, altar servers, or catechists. These ministries provide opportunities to serve both within the parish and the broader community.

- **Outreach to the Poor**: Many Catholic parishes run food pantries, shelters, and other outreach programs aimed at helping those in need. Volunteering in these programs is an excellent way to live out the call to service.

- **Catholic Charities**: **Catholic Charities** is a nationwide network of organizations that provide social services to those in need. Volunteers can work with these organizations to help people in their local communities.

- **Missionary Work**: For those with a sense of calling, **missionary work** within the Church can provide a deep and meaningful way to serve. This may include both local outreach or even international service, spreading the message of Christ through **evangelization**, **education**, or **humanitarian aid**.

Through service, Catholics are not only engaging with others but also living out the core values of their faith and helping to build a stronger Church community.

---

4. Joining Catholic Organizations and Groups

The Catholic Church offers a variety of organizations and groups where individuals can deepen their faith, form friendships, and contribute to the life of the Church.

Catholic Study Groups

- **Bible Study Groups**: Many parishes offer Bible study groups where Catholics can come together to explore Scripture, share insights, and grow in their knowledge of God's Word.

- **Catholic Social Groups**: Social groups and events provide opportunities for fellowship and community-building. These groups often include activities like retreats, dinners, and special celebrations, all aimed at fostering a sense of belonging.

- **Youth and Young Adult Ministries**: Many parishes have vibrant ministries specifically for youth and young adults, providing spaces for these groups to come together in fellowship, study, and service.

Catholic Lay Associations and Movements

- **The Knights of Columbus**: This fraternal service organization for men focuses on charity, unity, fraternity, and patriotism. It's an excellent avenue for men to become more involved in the life of the Church.
- **Catholic Women's Groups**: Women's groups often gather to offer spiritual formation, service opportunities, and fellowship for women in various stages of life.
- **Opus Dei, Legion of Mary, and Other Movements**: These are specialized organizations that help individuals grow spiritually and take on apostolic missions, often providing a structured way to live out the Catholic faith more intentionally.

Getting involved in these organizations is an effective way to become part of the larger Catholic family, grow in one's relationship with God, and serve others in the process.

---

5. Becoming Part of a Parish Community

The **parish** is the primary community where Catholics worship, learn, and serve together. Active participation in parish life is key to becoming deeply involved in the Catholic community. It offers a place for spiritual nourishment, fellowship, and service.

How to Get Involved in Your Parish

- **Attend Mass Regularly**: Regular attendance at Mass is the primary way to stay connected with your parish community and the larger Church.
- **Join Parish Activities**: Attend parish events like potlucks, festivals, and social gatherings to meet other members and build relationships.
- **Volunteer for Parish Committees**: Many parishes have committees for planning events, maintaining the building, or running programs. Volunteering on a parish committee allows individuals to make a tangible contribution to the life of the Church.
- **Participate in Parish Retreats**: Many parishes organize spiritual retreats throughout the year, offering an opportunity for reflection, prayer, and deepening one's faith.

The parish is the heart of the Catholic community, and becoming involved in its life strengthens both the individual and the entire body of Christ.

---

6. The Global Catholic Community

While local involvement is essential, being Catholic also means being part of the **universal Church**. The Catholic Church is **global**—spanning every continent, culture, and nation. Catholics are called to look beyond their immediate community and to see themselves as part of the **worldwide body of Christ**.

Opportunities for Global Involvement

- **Catholic Missions**: Engaging in or supporting **missionary efforts** helps to spread the Catholic faith and serve the global community. This may include support for Catholic missions overseas or participating in local outreach for international causes.

- **World Youth Day**: **World Youth Day** is an international event where young people from around the world gather to celebrate their faith and meet the Pope. It's an excellent opportunity to experience the universal nature of the Church.
- **Solidarity with the Poor**: The Church calls its members to engage in works of **social justice** on a global scale, including addressing issues like poverty, human rights, and the environment.

Becoming involved in the Catholic community also means embracing the call to global solidarity, joining with millions of other Catholics in service and witness to the Gospel.

Becoming involved in the Catholic community is an essential aspect of living out the faith. It is through the Church community that Catholics deepen their relationship with God, serve others, and grow spiritually. Whether through participation in the sacraments, volunteering, joining parish ministries, or connecting with Catholic organizations, there are countless ways to engage with the Church. Becoming an active member of the Catholic community is not just about individual spiritual growth; it is about contributing to the **mission of Christ** in the world, fostering unity, and living the Gospel in both word and deed. By engaging with others in the Church, Catholics find themselves united in a shared mission of love, service, and faith.

Lifelong Learning and Spiritual Growth

Catholicism teaches that the journey of faith is not a one-time event but a lifelong process of **learning**, **growing**, and **deepening** one's relationship with God. **Spiritual growth** is not only about acquiring knowledge but also about **transforming the heart** and **being shaped by God's grace**. The Church encourages its members to continuously seek **spiritual maturity**, continually striving to live out their faith with greater **intensity**, **purpose**, and **depth**.

Lifelong learning is essential in the Catholic faith. It goes beyond just formal education or doctrinal knowledge and touches on the way we experience and live out the mysteries of our faith. This chapter explores the idea of **lifelong learning** in the Catholic tradition and how it facilitates **spiritual growth**. By engaging in ongoing **formation**, **study**, and **reflection**, Catholics can continue to mature spiritually and better fulfill their **vocation** as disciples of Christ.

---

1. The Call to Lifelong Learning in the Catholic Tradition

Catholicism holds that **faith** and **knowledge** are intrinsically linked. The Church encourages its members to be lifelong learners, ever seeking a deeper understanding of their faith, both intellectually and spiritually. **Pope John Paul II** emphasized this when he wrote in *Fides et Ratio* (Faith and Reason) that faith and reason go hand in hand and that Catholics must continue to seek knowledge, engage in deep reflection, and use their reason to understand the mysteries of God.

Lifelong learning is rooted in the understanding that our faith is not static but dynamic. Just as our relationship with God evolves, so too does our understanding of His Word and how to live it out in the world. Catholics are called to continually grow in both **intellectual formation** (learning more about the **doctrines** of the Church) and **spiritual formation** (deepening one's **prayer life**, **virtues**, and **commitment to service**).

---

2. Spiritual Growth: Becoming More Like Christ

Spiritual growth is the process by which a person becomes more and more conformed to the image of Christ. The ultimate goal of Catholic life is to become more like Jesus in our thoughts, words, and deeds. This transformation is a work of **grace**, but it requires active participation on the part of the believer. As **St. Paul** writes in his letter to the Romans, "For those whom He foreknew He also predestined to be conformed to the image of His Son" (Romans 8:29).

Spiritual growth involves several key aspects:

- **Prayer and Meditation**: Regular prayer helps Catholics to cultivate a deeper intimacy with God. Personal reflection on Scripture (meditation) and participation in liturgical prayer (e.g., the Mass) provide the foundation for spiritual growth.
- **Virtue Development**: Growth in **virtue**, such as **humility**, **patience**, **charity**, and **fortitude**, is essential. As Catholics grow in virtue, they become more Christlike, reflecting His love in their relationships with others.
- **Sacramental Life**: Actively participating in the **sacraments** (particularly the **Eucharist** and **Reconciliation**) nourishes spiritual growth by bringing the individual closer to God and restoring grace when they fall short.

The call to spiritual growth is both individual and communal. Catholics grow spiritually by embracing both **personal devotion** and active **participation** in the communal life of the Church, such as through Mass, fellowship, and service to others.

---

3. The Role of Study in Lifelong Learning

In the Catholic Church, **study** is considered a vital part of **spiritual formation**. Catholics are encouraged to **study Scripture**, **Church**

doctrine, and the writings of the Church Fathers and theologians to deepen their understanding of their faith. Knowledge of these texts, paired with prayer and reflection, leads to greater **spiritual insight** and **wisdom**.

Sacred Scripture

The **Bible** is the foundational text of Catholicism, and lifelong learning involves developing a deeper understanding of its message. **Daily reading of Scripture**, whether alone or in a group setting, nurtures personal spiritual growth and helps believers better understand the **mysteries of faith**.

- **Lectio Divina**: This ancient practice of prayerful reading and reflection on Scripture encourages a deeper, more intimate relationship with the Word of God. It is an approach that allows the believer to internalize the truths of Scripture and apply them to everyday life.

Church Doctrine and Teachings

The **Catechism of the Catholic Church** serves as a guide to understanding the core beliefs and teachings of the Church. Catholics are encouraged to study the Catechism throughout their lives, as it provides clear and comprehensive explanations of the faith.

- **Doctrinal Study**: Understanding fundamental concepts such as the **Trinity**, **salvation**, **grace**, and **the sacraments** allows Catholics to deepen their intellectual grasp of the faith and be more effective in living out their vocation.

The Writings of the Saints and Theologians

The writings of great saints and theologians offer insights into the depths of the Catholic faith. Figures like **St. Augustine**, **St. Thomas Aquinas**, **St. Teresa of Avila**, and **St. John Paul II** have left behind rich theological reflections that help the believer to understand God's revelation more fully.

- **Spiritual Classics**: Reading the writings of saints and mystics deepens one's spiritual life and provides examples of holiness to follow.

---

4. Faith Formation through Prayer and Reflection

A critical component of lifelong learning in the Catholic tradition is **prayer**. **St. John Paul II** wrote that **prayer** is "the soul of the Christian life." Catholics are called to pray regularly, not only as a way to communicate with God but also to help cultivate deeper spiritual awareness and transformation.

Personal Prayer Life

- **Daily Prayer**: Catholics are encouraged to pray daily, using personal prayer, such as the **Rosary**, **morning and evening prayers**, or spontaneous prayers, to foster a continual relationship with God.

- **Spiritual Direction**: Seeking guidance from a **spiritual director** can be an essential part of the spiritual journey. A spiritual director helps individuals to reflect on their prayer life, discern God's will, and grow in holiness.

Contemplation and Meditation

In addition to vocal prayer, Catholics are also encouraged to practice **contemplation** and **meditation**—reflecting deeply on God's presence, His Word, and His works in their lives. These practices help develop **spiritual maturity** and cultivate a deep awareness of God's love and action in the world.

---

5. The Importance of Community in Lifelong Learning

Spiritual growth and lifelong learning are not meant to be pursued in isolation. The **Catholic community** plays a significant role in helping individuals grow in faith. As **St. Paul** reminds the early Christians, "We are many parts, but one body" (1 Corinthians 12:12). The Church is a community where individuals can share knowledge, grow in faith, and support one another in their journey toward holiness.

Parish Involvement

Being an active participant in a **parish** allows individuals to connect with other Catholics and learn from their experiences. Regular attendance at **Mass**, participation in **Bible studies**, joining **ministry groups**, and volunteering in parish programs are all ways to foster lifelong learning in the context of community.

Catholic Organizations and Retreats

Catholic **organizations** and **retreats** also provide opportunities for spiritual and intellectual growth. Retreats allow individuals to take time away from daily distractions and immerse themselves in prayer, reflection, and formation. These experiences can deepen one's faith and inspire a renewed commitment to lifelong learning.

---

6. Lifelong Service as a Means of Growth

Service is an essential part of spiritual growth. Serving others is a concrete way of living out the Catholic faith and growing in **humility**, **charity**, and **selflessness**.

Serving in the Church and Beyond

- **Volunteer Work**: Serving in various ministries, such as **teaching catechism**, **working with the poor**, or helping at the parish, allows individuals to practice the faith they are learning.
- **Missionary Work**: Lifelong learning is not limited to study alone; it is deeply connected to **mission**. Catholics are encouraged to engage in **evangelization**, whether through local or international

missionary work, as part of their lifelong commitment to service.

---

7. The Role of Scripture and Catholic Literature in Lifelong Learning

Catholicism encourages lifelong engagement with Scripture and Catholic literature. Catholics are encouraged to read the **Bible** regularly, and there is also a rich body of Catholic literature—spiritual books, encyclicals, and documents—that helps guide the faithful in their spiritual formation.

Catholic Books and Spiritual Literature

- **Encyclicals**: Documents written by the Pope, such as *Deus Caritas Est* or *Evangelii Gaudium*, help Catholics understand contemporary issues from a Catholic perspective and grow in their faith.

- **Spiritual Reading**: Books written by spiritual authors, saints, or theologians provide practical insights into living the faith and growing in holiness.

Lifelong learning and spiritual growth are essential to the Catholic life. Faith is a journey that continues throughout one's life, and Catholics are encouraged to engage in continual study, prayer, reflection, and service to grow deeper in their relationship with God and others. Spiritual growth is not a destination but an ongoing process of **conversion**, **learning**, and **transformation**. By committing to lifelong learning, Catholics are not only able to better understand the mysteries of faith but also able to live out those mysteries in their everyday lives. This journey toward holiness and deepening faith is ultimately a response to God's **love**, and it requires both personal effort and community support.

Continuing the Journey of Faith

The journey of faith is not a singular event but a **lifelong pilgrimage** toward deeper communion with God. It is a process that encompasses **learning**, **growth**, and **transformation**—one that never truly ends. From the moment of **baptism** to the final encounter with God in the eternal life to come, Catholics are invited to embrace a dynamic, ever-evolving relationship with Christ, His Church, and the world. This journey is marked by moments of profound grace, challenges that strengthen faith, and a continual unfolding of **God's love** in every aspect of life.

In the Catholic tradition, faith is not merely a personal pursuit; it is also a communal experience. The Church, through its rich sacraments, teachings, and community life, accompanies each believer on their path. It is through the Church that we are sustained, guided, and challenged to live out the faith with both **devotion** and **action**. As Catholics, we are called to engage in **prayer**, **study**, **service**, and **sacramental life** as means of deepening our relationship with God and growing in holiness.

Faith as a Lifelong Journey

Throughout this book, we have explored the various dimensions of Catholic life—its beliefs, practices, and call to holiness. At the heart of all these practices lies an invitation: **to continue the journey of faith**. This journey involves **constant conversion**, or **metanoia**, a daily turning toward God and away from sin. It involves the deepening of virtues such as **charity**, **patience**, and **humility**, which help the believer reflect more of Christ in their life.

The journey of faith also invites Catholics to **participate in the life of the Church**—to be an active member of the community that worships, serves, and grows together in faith. It is a call to **continue learning**, as **spiritual formation** and **intellectual growth** never cease. As Catholics, we are encouraged to remain humble and open to the Holy Spirit's work in us, recognizing that our understanding of God and our relationship with Him will continually deepen.

Growing in the Sacraments

Central to continuing the journey of faith is an ongoing engagement with the **sacraments**. These sacred rituals are not merely rites to be performed but living encounters with **God's grace**. **Baptism** initiates us into the Christian life, **Eucharist** sustains us, **Reconciliation** heals us, and **Confirmation** strengthens us for service. These sacraments are the means through which we grow in our relationship with God and receive the grace necessary to navigate the challenges of life.

The sacramental life also points toward the ultimate goal of the Catholic journey: **eternal communion with God**. By continually participating in the sacraments, Catholics are empowered to live holy lives that witness to God's presence in the world. Each sacrament is an opportunity to deepen one's commitment to Christ and to the Church, allowing believers to move closer to the vision of **heavenly life**.

A Community of Faith

Catholicism is not meant to be lived in isolation. As the Church teaches, **we are members of one body**, called to support one another and grow together. The Church, with its rich history, traditions, and community life, serves as both a guide and a **source of strength**. Whether through the regular **celebration of the Mass**, **participation in parish ministries**, or involvement in Catholic organizations, believers find support and encouragement from others who are on the same journey.

The **Catholic community** is not limited to those in the local parish; it extends throughout the entire world. Catholics are connected through the universal Church, and this global communion reminds each member that their faith is part of something much larger than themselves. Whether through **mission work**, **social justice efforts**, or simply sharing the faith with others, Catholics are always called to witness Christ's love in the world.

Responding to the Call to Holiness

At the heart of the Catholic journey is a call to **holiness**. This is not about perfection or attaining spiritual success but about a **heartfelt desire** to live in union with God, to become more like Christ. The **saints**, who have gone before us, are models of this holiness. Their lives were not without struggle, but their response to God's grace led them to extraordinary lives of virtue, charity, and devotion.

Holiness is expressed in everyday acts of **love**, **service**, and **sacrifice**. Whether caring for the sick, helping a neighbor, or praying for the world, every act of kindness and devotion contributes to the journey toward God. The Church encourages every Catholic, regardless of age or station in life, to pursue holiness in their particular state of life. Whether married, single, ordained, or consecrated, each person is called to a specific **vocation** that is a pathway to sanctity.

The Final Destination: Eternal Life with God

The ultimate goal of the Catholic journey is the **eternal union with God** in **heaven**. This union is not a passive reward but the fulfillment of all that has been promised through Christ. The journey toward God, while begun here on earth, continues beyond death, when the faithful will experience the fullness of God's presence in eternal life.

The path to heaven is one of continual **growth** and **transformation**, shaped by a lifetime of **faithful service** and **obedience**. While the journey may include struggles, trials, and doubts, it is also filled with moments of grace, joy, and peace. Ultimately, the journey is one of **hope**, knowing that through the death and resurrection of Christ, the faithful have the promise of eternal life.

The journey of faith is a call to continually grow, learn, and deepen one's relationship with God. It is not just a path to be followed once but a lifelong commitment to be shaped by **God's love**, **grace**, and **truth**. As Catholics, we are invited to embrace this journey with an open heart, continually seeking **holiness**, participating in the **sacraments**, and living out our faith in **community**. Though the road may be long and at times difficult, the ultimate destination is one of **eternal joy** in the presence of God. As we continue our journey, we trust that the Holy Spirit will guide us, and the love of Christ will sustain us, leading us to the fullness of life with God.

Printed in Dunstable, United Kingdom

74517041R00112